EZEKIEL

Redemption for God's People

John MacArthur

Harper*Christian*
Resources

MacArthur Bible Studies
Ezekiel: Redemption for God's People
© 2024 by John MacArthur

Published in Grand Rapids, Michigan, by HarperChristian Resources. HarperChristian Resources is a registered trademark of HarperCollins Christian Publishing, Inc.

Requests for information should be sent to customercare@harpercollins.com.

ISBN 978-0-310-12384-2 (softcover)
ISBN 978-0-310-12385-9 (ebook)

HarperChristian Resources titles may be purchased in bulk for church, business, fundraising, or ministry use. For information, please e-mail ResourceSpecialist@ChurchSource.com.

"Unleashing God's Truth, One Verse at a Time ®" is a trademark of Grace to You. All rights reserved.

Some material from the Introduction, "Keys to the Text," and "Exploring the Meaning" sections are taken from *The MacArthur Bible Commentary*, John MacArthur. Copyright © 2005 Thomas Nelson Publishers.

First Printing November 2024 / Printed in the United States of America

24 25 26 27 28 LBC 5 4 3 2 1

CONTENTS

Contents

INTRODUCTION

When we think about the Old Testament prophets, it is easy to categorize them in terms of "before" and "after." Many prophets received and declared the word of the Lord *before* specific historical events came to pass—even centuries before. They offered warnings of future judgment and promises of future blessing. Other prophets declared God's word *after* significant events had taken place. They helped God's people process those events from His perspective, offering comfort or confrontation as the Israelites attempted to move forward.

Ezekiel is an interesting figure among the prophets in that his ministry took place "during" the significant events that are the primary focus of his prophetic work. Ezekiel and his wife (mentioned in 24:15–27) were among ten thousand Jews taken captive to Babylon in 597 BC (see 2 Kings 24:11–18). They lived in Tel Abib (see Ezekiel 3:15) on the bank of the Chebar River, probably southeast of Babylon. Ezekiel's prophetic words were spoken to Jewish exiles and to those still living in and around Jerusalem. He offered commentary on critical events as they were happening and declared God's warnings of further consequences in the immediate future—namely, the siege and ultimate destruction of Jerusalem.

To be clear, there are portions of Ezekiel's prophecy that point farther into the future—including a lengthy vision in which Ezekiel describes the dimensions of God's future temple to be built during the millennial reign of Christ. But God's decision to equip and instruct His prophet in the immediate context of the Babylonian conquest of Israel shows His love and care for His people even during that difficult time. Employing striking visuals and with poignant moments, the book of Ezekiel reveals God's divine glory and His deep love for His people.

AUTHOR AND DATE

The book has always been named for its author, Ezekiel (see 1:3; 24:24), who is nowhere else mentioned in Scripture. His name means "strengthened by God," which he indeed was for the ministry to which God called him (see 3:8–9). Ezekiel uses visions, prophecies, parables, signs, and symbols to proclaim and dramatize the message of God to His exiled people.

If the "thirtieth year" of 1:1 refers to Ezekiel's age, he was twenty-five when taken captive and thirty when called into ministry. Thirty was the age when priests began their office, so it was a notable year for Ezekiel. His ministry began in 593/592 BC and extended at least twenty-two years until 571/570 BC (see 29:17). He was a contemporary of both Jeremiah (who was about twenty years older) and Daniel (who was about the same age), the latter of whom he names in 14:14, 20; 28:3 as an already well-known prophet. Like Jeremiah (see Jeremiah 1:1) and Zechariah (see Zechariah 1:1; Nehemiah 12:16), Ezekiel was a prophet and a priest (see Ezekiel 1:3). Because of his priestly background, he was particularly interested in and familiar with the temple details, so God used him to write about them (see 8:1–11:25; 40:1–47:12).

Ezekiel received his call to prophesy in 593 BC (see 1:2), in Babylon ("the land of the Chaldeans"), during the fifth year of King Jehoiachin's captivity, which began in 597 BC. Frequently, Ezekiel dates his prophecies from 597 BC (see 8:1; 20:1; 24:1; 26:1; 29:1; 30:20; 31:1; 32:1, 17; 33:21; 40:1). He also dates the message in Ezekiel 40:1 at 573/572 BC, the fourteenth year after 586 BC, which was the date of Jerusalem's final fall. The last dated utterance of Ezekiel was in 571/570 BC (see 29:17). Prophecies in Ezekiel 1–28 are in chronological order. In Ezekiel 29:1, the prophet regresses to a year earlier than in 26:1. But from 30:1 on (see 31:1; 32:1, 17), he is close to being strictly chronological.

BACKGROUND AND SETTING

From the historical perspective, Israel's united kingdom lasted more than 110 years (c. 1043–931 BC), through the reigns of Saul, David, and Solomon. The divided kingdom, Israel (north) and Judah (south), then extended from 931 BC to 722/721 BC. Israel fell to Assyria in 722/721 BC, leaving Judah the surviving kingdom for 135 years, until it fell to Babylon in 605–586 BC.

In the more immediate setting, several features were strategic. Politically, Assyria's vaunted military might had crumbled after 626 BC and its capital, Nineveh, was destroyed in 612 BC by the Babylonians and Medes (as related in the book of Nahum). The Neo-Babylonian Empire had flexed its muscles since Nabopolassar took the throne in 625 BC, and Egypt, under Pharaoh Necho II, was determined to conquer what she could. Babylon smashed Assyria in 612–605 BC and registered a decisive victory against Egypt in 605 BC at Carchemish, leaving no survivors according to the Babylonian Chronicle.

Also in 605 BC, Babylon, led by Nebuchadnezzar, began the conquest of Jerusalem and the deportation of captives, among them Daniel (see Daniel 1:2). In December of 598 BC, Nebuchadnezzar again besieged Jerusalem, and on March 16 of 597 BC, he took possession of it. This time, he took captive Jehoiachin and a group of ten thousand, including Ezekiel (see 2 Kings 24:11–18). The final destruction of Jerusalem and the conquest of Judah, including the third deportation, came in 586 BC.

Religiously, King Josiah (c. 640–609 BC) had instituted reforms in Judah (see 2 Chronicles 34). Tragically, despite his effort, idolatry had so dulled the Judeans that their overall awakening was only skin-deep. The Egyptian army killed Josiah as it crossed Palestine in 609 BC, and the Jews continued on in sin, racing toward judgment under Jehoahaz (609 BC), Jehoiakim (Eliakim) (609–598 BC), Jehoiachin (598–597 BC), and Zedekiah (597–586 BC).

Domestically, Ezekiel and the ten thousand exiles lived in Babylonia (see 2 Kings 24:14), more as colonists than captives, being permitted to farm tracts of land under somewhat favorable conditions (see Jeremiah 29). Ezekiel even had his own house (see 3:24; 20:1).

Prophetically, false prophets deceived the exiles with assurances of a speedy return to Judah (see 13:3, 16; Jeremiah 29:1). From 593–585 BC, Ezekiel warned that their beloved Jerusalem would be destroyed and their exile prolonged, so that there was no hope of immediate return. In 585 BC, an escapee from Jerusalem, who had evaded the Babylonians, reached Ezekiel with the first news that the city had fallen in 586 BC, about six months earlier (see Ezekiel 33:21). This dashed the false hopes of any immediate deliverance for the exiles, so the remainder of Ezekiel's prophecies relate to Israel's future restoration to its homeland and the final blessings of the messianic kingdom.

HISTORICAL AND THEOLOGICAL THEMES

The "glory of the Lord" is central to Ezekiel, appearing in 1:28; 3:12, 23; 10:4, 18; 11:23; 43:4–5; 44:4. The book includes graphic descriptions of the disobedience of Israel and Judah despite God's kindness (see chapter 23; cf. chapter

16). It shows that God desired for Israel to bear fruit that He could bless; however, the selfish indulgence of Judah left them ready for judgment, like a torched vine (see chapter 15). References are plentiful to Israel's idolatry and its consequences, such as Pelatiah dropping dead (see 11:13), a symbolic illustration of overall disaster for the people.

Many picturesque scenes illustrate the spiritual principles. Among these are Ezekiel eating a scroll (see Ezekiel 2); the faces on four angels representing aspects of creation over which God rules (see 1:10); a "barbershop" scene (see 5:1–4); graffiti on the temple walls, reminding readers of what God really wants in His dwelling place—namely, holiness and not ugliness (see 8:10); and sprinkled hot coals, depicting judgment (see 10:2, 7).

Chief among the theological themes are God's holiness and sovereignty. These are conveyed by frequent contrast of His bright glory against the despicable backdrop of Judah's sins (see 1:26–28; chapters 8–11; 43:1–7). Closely related is God's purpose of glorious triumph so that all may "know that I am the LORD." This divine monogram, God's signature authenticating His acts, is mentioned more than sixty times, usually with a judgment (see 6:7; 7:4), but occasionally after the promised restoration (see 34:27; 36:11, 38; 39:28).

Another feature involves God's angels carrying out His program behind the scenes (see 1:5–25; 10:1–22). A further important theme is God's holding each individual accountable for pursuing righteousness (see 18:3–32). Ezekiel also emphasizes sinfulness in Israel (see 2:3–7; 8:9–10) and other nations (see chapters 25–32). He deals with the necessity of God's wrath to deal with sin (see 7:1–8; 15:8); God's frustration of man's devices to escape from besieged Jerusalem (see 12:1–13; Jeremiah 39:4–7); and God's grace pledged in the Abrahamic covenant (see Genesis 12:1–3) being fulfilled by restoring Abraham's people to the land of the covenant (see Ezekiel 34; 36–48; Genesis 12:7). God promises to preserve a remnant of Israelites through whom He will fulfill His restoration promises and keep His inviolate Word.

INTERPRETIVE CHALLENGES

Ezekiel uses extensive symbolic language, as did the prophets Isaiah and Jeremiah. This raises the question as to whether certain portions of Ezekiel's writings are to be taken literally or figuratively. For example, being bound with ropes (see 3:25); whether the prophet was taken bodily to Jerusalem (see 8:1–3); how individual judgment can be worked out in Ezekiel 18 when the wicked elude death in 14:22–23 and some of the godly die in an invasion in 21:3–4; how God would permit a faithful prophet's wife to die (see 24:15–27); when some of the judgments on other nations will occur (see chapters 25–32); whether the temple described in chapters 40–46 will be a literal one and in what form; and how promises of Israel's future relate to God's program with the church. These issues will be discussed in this study guide.

The book of Ezekiel can primarily be divided into sections about condemnation/retribution and then consolation/restoration. A more detailed look divides the book into four sections. First, there are prophecies on the ruin of Jerusalem (chapters 1–24). Second, prophecies of retribution on nearby nations are detailed (chapters 25–32), with a glimpse at God's future restoration of Israel (see 28:25–26). Third, there is a transition chapter (33) that gives instruction concerning a last call for Israel to repent. Finally, the fourth division includes rich expectations involving God's future restoration of Israel (chapters 34–48).

A Vision and a Commission
Ezekiel 1:1–3:27

Drawing Near

Do you have an adequate view of God? What do your day-to-day thoughts of God reveal about your estimation of His glory?

_____

_____

_____

_____

_____

_____

_____

_____

_____

_____

_____

_____

_____

The Context

The phrase "shock and awe" was introduced to American culture during the second war with Iraq in 2003. The phrase could also apply to the opening chapter of Ezekiel's book, which is filled with a stunning visual display of God's glory and divine presence. This display includes a whirlwind filled with "raging fire" (1:4), radiantly colored angelic beings "in appearance like a flash of lightning" (verse 14), and a stunning vision of God seated on a throne of sapphire, surrounded by "the appearance of the likeness of the glory of the Lord" (verse 28).

The immediate context of this glorious vision was Ezekiel's call as a prophet. The visual representation of angelic beings in God's presence (verses 4–14) and the display of His majestic throne (verses 15–28) offered assurance to Ezekiel that he was indeed receiving word from the God of Abraham, Isaac, and Jacob. That assurance was no doubt helpful for the prophet to retain his resolve while carrying out a difficult assignment over the course of decades.

Chapters 2 and 3 offer specific details about that assignment. God commissioned Ezekiel to speak with the children of Israel, "a rebellious nation" (2:3). Ezekiel would experience physical hardships along with social pressure and rejection during his ministry as a "watchman" (3:17). For that reason, the Lord strengthened Ezekiel at the beginning of his ministry and committed to continue fortifying him over the long years: "Behold, I have made your face strong against their faces, and your forehead strong against their foreheads. Like adamant stone, harder than flint, I have made your forehead; do not be afraid of them, nor be dismayed at their looks, though they are a rebellious house" (3:8–9).

KEYS TO THE TEXT

Read Ezekiel 1:1–3:27, noting the key words and phrases indicated below.

A Divine Appearance: The opening vision that Ezekiel relates in his book focuses on angels surrounding God's presence and the glory of God's throne in heaven.

1:1. THIRTIETH YEAR: Most likely this was Ezekiel's age, since the date relative to the king's reign is given in 1:2. Thirty was the age when a priest (see verse 3) began his priestly duties (see Numbers 4).

VISIONS OF GOD: This scene has similarities to the visions of God's throne in Isaiah 6 and Revelation 4–5, where the emphasis is also on a glimpse of that throne just before judgment is released. The term "vision" (see Ezekiel 8:3; 11:24; 40:2; 43:3) is derived from a Hebrew verb meaning "to see." Dreams and visions were often recognized by the ancients as revelations from the gods, or from God Himself, in the case of the Hebrews (see Isaiah 1:1).

River Chebar: A major canal off of the Euphrates River, south of Babylon.

2. FIFTH YEAR: This is 593 BC. The king, Ezekiel, and 10,000 others (see 2 Kings 24:14) had been deported to Babylon in 597 BC. Ezekiel was age twenty-five at the time.

3. WORD OF THE LORD . . . HAND OF THE LORD: Just as God had prepared Isaiah (see Isaiah 6:5–13) and Jeremiah (see Jeremiah 1:4–19), so the Lord prepares Ezekiel to receive revelation and strengthens him for his high and arduous task to speak as His prophet.

EZEKIEL THE PRIEST: See note on verse 1.

4. WHIRLWIND . . . FIRE: Judgment on Judah, in a further and totally devastating phase (beyond the 597 BC deportation) is to come out of the north, and later did come from Babylon in 588–586 BC (see Jeremiah 39–40). Its terror is depicted by a fiery whirlwind emblematic of God's judgments and the golden brightness signifying God's dazzling glory.

5. FOUR LIVING CREATURES: Four angels, most likely the cherubs in Ezekiel 10:1–22, appearing in the erect posture and figure of man (note face, legs, feet, and hands in verses 6–8) emerge to serve God who judges. The number four may have respect to the four corners of the earth, implying that God's angels execute His commands everywhere.

6. FOUR FACES: See note on verse 10.

FOUR WINGS: Four wings instead of two symbolize an emphasis on speed in performing God's will (see verse 14).

7. LEGS: They were not bent like an animal's but "straight" like pillars, showing strength.

CALVES' FEET: This points to their stability and firm stance.

8. HANDS OF A MAN: This is symbolic of their skillful service.

9. DID NOT TURN: They were able to move in any direction without needing to first turn, giving swift access to do God's will. Apparently, all were synchronized as to the way they moved (see verse 12).

10. FACES: These symbols identify the angels as intelligent ("man"), powerful ("lion"), servile ("ox"), and swift ("eagle").

12. THE SPIRIT: This refers to the divine impulse by which God moved them to do His will (see verse 20).

13. LIKE . . . FIRE . . . TORCHES: Their appearance conveyed God's glory and pure, burning justice (see Isaiah 6), which they assisted in carrying out even on Israel, who had for so long hardened themselves against His patience.

14. RAN BACK AND FORTH; Intense, relentless motion signifies God's constant work of judgment.

15. A WHEEL: This depicts God's judgment as a war machine (like a massive chariot) moving where He is to judge. The cherubim above the ark are called chariots in 1 Chronicles 28:18.

16. WHEEL IN THE MIDDLE OF A WHEEL: This depicts the gigantic (verse 15, "on the earth" and "so high," verse 18) energy of the complicated revolutions of God's massive judgment machinery bringing about His purposes with unerring certainty.

17. DID NOT TURN ASIDE. The judgment machine moved where the angels went (see verses 19–20).

18. EYES: These may picture God's omniscience (His perfect knowledge) given to these angelic servants so they can act unerringly in judgment. God does nothing by blind impulse.

20. SPIRIT: See note on verse 12.

24. NOISE OF MANY WATERS: This imagery could have in mind a thunderous rush of heavy rain or the crashing of surf on rocks (see Ezekiel 43:2; Revelation 1:15; 14:2; 19:6).

25. VOICE: No doubt this is the "voice of the Almighty" (verse 24), since God's throne was "over their heads."

26. A THRONE: From everlasting to everlasting, God has always ruled over all things (see Psalm 11:4; 47:1–9; 103:19; 148:8–13; Revelation 4:2–8). This universal kingdom is to be distinguished from God's mediatorial kingdom on earth.

THE APPEARANCE OF A MAN: The Godhead appears in the likeness of humanity, though God is a spirit (see John 4:24). The Messiah, God incarnate, is the representative of the "fullness of the Godhead" (Colossians 2:9); thus, this can be a prelude to the Incarnation of the Messiah in His character as Savior and Judge (see Revelation 19:11–16).

28. GLORY: This term is derived from a Hebrew verb that is used to describe the weight or worthiness of something. It can refer to something negative, such as the severe degree of sin in the city of Sodom that had reached the point of making it worthy of destruction (see Genesis 18:20). However, the word usually depicts greatness and splendor. God's glory is described in the Old Testament as taking the form of a cloud (see Exodus 24:15–18) and filling the temple (see 1 Kings 8:11). The appropriate response to God's glory is to reverence Him by bowing before Him, as Ezekiel did (see 3:23; 43:3). God's glory

shines fully in the person of Jesus Christ (see 2 Corinthians 4:6), which is a constant theme in Ezekiel.

FELL ON MY FACE: John, in Revelation 1:17, had the same reaction on seeing the glory of the Lord.

A DIVINE ASSIGNMENT: *This section in Ezekiel pictures the selective empowering by the Holy Spirit to equip an individual for special service to the Lord. What God commands a servant to do, He gives the enabling power to do by His Spirit.*

2:1. SON OF MAN: A term used more than ninety times by Ezekiel to indicate his humanness. The term serves both to emphasize the difference between God the Creator and His creatures and to mark the prophet Ezekiel as a representative member of the human race. Ezekiel's life was a living parable or object lesson to the Hebrew captives in Babylon (see 1:3; 3:4–7). In word and deed, Ezekiel was a sign to the house of Israel (see 12:6). Jesus adopted the title "Son of Man" because He, too, was a representative person—the "last Adam" who became a life-giving spirit (see Matthew 8:20; 1 Corinthians 15:45). The title "Son of Man" also alludes to Daniel's vision of the heavenly being who is "like the Son of Man" (Daniel 7:13). Thus, the title highlights the mystery of the Incarnation—the fact that Christ is both divine and human. As the God-man, Jesus became a glorious sign for all of sinful humanity (see Luke 2:34).

2. THE SPIRIT ENTERED ME: This selective empowering by the Holy Spirit occurred frequently in the Old Testament (see Ezekiel 11:5; 37:1; Numbers 24:2; Judges 3:10; 6:34; 11:29; 13:25; 1 Samuel 10:10; 16:13–14; 19:20; 2 Chronicles 15:1; Luke 4:18).

5. WHETHER THEY HEAR: The people cannot plead ignorance.

PROPHET: This term probably comes from the Hebrew root word meaning "to announce" or "to proclaim" (see Jeremiah 19:14; 37:7–9). Another possible derivation is from a Hebrew word meaning "to bubble up" or "to pour forth." Prophecy can be compared to the "bubbling up" of the Holy Spirit in a person who delivers a divine message (see Amos 3:8; Micah 3:8). In Old Testament times, prophets were heralds or spokesmen who delivered a message for someone else (see 2 Kings 17:13). In the case of the Hebrew prophets, they spoke for God. This is the reason the prophets introduced their messages with "thus says the LORD of hosts" on countless occasions (see, for example, Jeremiah 9:7, 17).

6. BRIERS AND THORNS . . . SCORPIONS: See Ezekiel 3:7, 9; 22:29. God used these figures of speech to describe the people of Judah whose obstinate rejection of His Word was like the barbs of thorns and stings of scorpions to Ezekiel. The wicked were often so called (see 2 Samuel 23:6; Song of Songs 2:2; Isaiah 9:18).

8. OPEN YOUR MOUTH AND EAT WHAT I GIVE YOU: Ezekiel was to obey the command by not literally eating a scroll (verses 9–10) but in a spiritual sense by receiving God's message so that it became an inward passion. (See also Ezekiel 3:1–3, 10; Jeremiah 15:16.)

10. WRITING ON THE INSIDE AND . . . OUTSIDE: Scrolls were normally written on one side only, but this judgment message was so full it required all the available space (see Zechariah 5:3; Revelation 5:1) to chronicle the suffering and sorrow that sin had brought, as recorded in Ezekiel 2–32.

> A DIVINE RESPONSIBILITY: *This section describes Ezekiel's responsibility as a prophet of the Lord. It reveals that what God commands, He gives the sufficiency to do.*

3:1–3. EAT THIS SCROLL . . . SO I ATE: God's messenger must first internalize God's truth for himself, then preach it.

3. LIKE HONEY: Even though the message was judgment on Israel, the scroll was sweet because it was God's Word (see Psalms 19:10; 119:103) and because it vindicated God in holiness, righteousness, glory, and faithfulness, in which Jeremiah also delighted (see Jeremiah 15:16). Bitterness also was experienced by the prophet (see Ezekiel 3:14) in this message of judgment confronting Judah's rebellion (see verse 9). The apostle John records a similar bittersweet experience with the Word of God in Revelation 10:9–10.

7. THEY WILL NOT LISTEN TO ME: See John 15:20.

8–9. I HAVE MADE YOUR FACE STRONG: God will enable the prophet to live up to his name, which means "strengthened by God" (see Ezekiel 2:2; 3:14, 24; Isaiah 41:10; Jeremiah 1:8, 17).

9. A REBELLIOUS HOUSE: It is sad to observe that the exile and affliction did not make the Jews more responsive to God; rather, they were hardened by their sufferings. God gave Ezekiel a corresponding "hardness" to sustain his ministry as prophet to the exiles.

12, 14. THE SPIRIT LIFTED ME UP: This phrase describes the prophet being elevated to a heavenly vision, as in the experiences of Ezekiel 8:3; 11:1.

14. BITTERNESS: See note on verse 3.

15. THE CAPTIVES: Tel Abib was the main city for the Jewish captives, who may have included some of the ten tribes taken long before in the conquering of the northern kingdom of Israel in 722 BC. Second Kings 17:6 may indicate this ("Habor" is the same river as Chebar).

REMAINED . . . SEVEN DAYS: Ezekiel sat with the sorrowing people for seven days, the usual period for showing deep grief (see Job 2:13). He identified with them in their suffering (see Psalm 137:1), thus trying to win their trust when he spoke God's word.

17. A WATCHMAN: This role was spiritually analogous to the role of a watchmen on a city wall, vigilant to spot the approach of an enemy and warn the residents to muster a defense. The prophet gave timely warnings of approaching judgment. The work of a watchman is vividly set forth in 2 Samuel 18:24–27 and 2 Kings 9:17–20. (See notes on Ezekiel 33:1–20.)

18. THE WICKED . . . HIM . . . HIS: The emphasis of singular pronouns is on individuals. The ministries of Habakkuk (see 2:1), Jeremiah (see 6:17), and Isaiah (see 56:10) were more national than individual. Ezekiel's ministry was more personal, focused on individual responsibility to trust and obey God. Disobedience or obedience to God's messages was a matter of life or death. Ezekiel 18:1–20 is particularly devoted to this emphasis.

NO WARNING . . . DIE: People are not to assume that ignorance, even owing to the negligence of preachers, will be any excuse to save them from divine punishment (see Romans 2:12).

SAVE HIS LIFE: This refers to physical death, not eternal damnation, though that would be a consequence for many. In the Pentateuch, God had commanded death for many violations of His law and warned that it could be a consequence of any consistent sin (see Joshua 1:16–18). The people of Israel had long abandoned that severe standard of purification, so God took execution back into His own hands, as in the destruction of Israel, Judah, and Jerusalem. On the other hand, God had also promised special protection and life to the obedient (see Ezekiel 18:9–32; 33:11–16; Proverbs 4:4; 7:2; Amos 5:4, 6).

18, 20. HIS BLOOD I WILL REQUIRE: Although each sinner is responsible for his own sin (see Ezekiel 18:1–20), the prophet who is negligent in his duty to proclaim the warning message becomes, in God's sight, a manslayer when God takes that person's life. The responsibility of the prophet is serious (see James 3:1), and he is responsible for that person's death in the sense of Genesis 9:5. The apostle

Paul had this passage (and Ezekiel 33:6, 8) in view in Acts 18:6 and 20:26. Even for contemporary preachers, there is such a warning in Hebrews 13:17. Certainly the consequence for such unfaithfulness on the preacher's part includes divine chastening and loss of eternal reward (see 1 Corinthians 4:1–5).

20. A RIGHTEOUS MAN: Here is a person who was obeying God by doing what was right but then fell into sin, and God took his life in chastisement. The "stumbling block" was a stone of judgment that kills. Psalm 119:165 announces, "Great peace have those who love Your law, and nothing causes them to stumble." The crushing stone always falls on the disobedient. Hebrews 12:9 reports it is better to obey and "live." (See 1 Corinthians 11:30; James 1:21; 1 John 5:16.)

21. DELIVERED YOUR SOUL: The prophet had done his duty.

24. SHUT YOURSELF INSIDE YOUR HOUSE: Ezekiel was to fulfill much of his ministry at home (see Ezekiel 8:1; 12:1–7), thereby limiting it to those who came to hear him there.

25. THEY WILL PUT ROPES ON YOU: These were not literal ropes but spiritual. On one hand, they could be the inner ropes of depressing influence that the rebellious Jews exerted on his spirit. Their perversity, like ropes, would repress his freedom in preaching. More likely, they implied the restraint that God placed on him by supernatural power so that he could only go and speak where and when God chose (see verses 26–27).

26–27. YOU SHALL BE MUTE: Ezekiel was not to speak primarily but to act out God's message. The prohibition was only partial, for on any occasion when God did open his mouth, as He often did in Ezekiel 5–7, he was to speak (see 3:22; 11:25; 12:10, 19, 23, 28). The end of such intermittent muteness with regard to his own people closely paralleled Ezekiel's receiving a refugee's (or refugees') report of Jerusalem's fall (see 24:25–27; 33:21–22). He also spoke about judgments on other nations (see Ezekiel 25–32).

UNLEASHING THE TEXT

1) What do you learn about God's nature from Ezekiel 1:4–28?

2) In Ezekiel 1:4–14, the prophet describes the angelic beings in the presence of God. What does this passage, and the Bible as a whole, teach about what angels are and what they do?

_____

_____

_____

_____

_____

_____

3) How would you summarize the assignment that God gave to Ezekiel in chapters 2 and 3? What was Ezekiel called to be and what was he to do?

_____

_____

_____

_____

_____

_____

4) The Spirit of God features prominently in these chapters. What does this section reveal about the work of the Holy Spirit?

_____

_____

_____

_____

_____

_____

EXPLORING THE MEANING

Glory is a key attribute of God's nature. One of the functions of the Bible is to reveal truths about God, including those about His nature. For example, we know from Scripture that God is love (see 1 John 4:7–8), that He is unchanging (see Malachi 3:6), that He is wise (see Romans 11:33), that He is good (see Psalm 34:8), that He is gracious and merciful (see Psalm 145:8), and that He is just (see Deuteronomy 32:4). In a similar way, the first chapter of Ezekiel offers a detailed glimpse into the aspect of God's nature that we call "glory." God is glorious, and He revealed that glory to Ezekiel through an incredible vision. Importantly, it is not that God *displayed* glory in this chapter or *acted* in ways that are glorious, for that would imply that God reflected something glorious that was outside of Himself. Instead, the text shows that God *is* glory. Glory is His nature, and that glory is sourced entirely in Him. Another way to express this truth is that we can only learn about glory (or experience it) by looking to God and studying Him as the source of all that is glorious.

God calls His people to serve Him. Chapters 2 and 3 of Ezekiel's prophecy set the stage for the rest of the book by describing God's call for Ezekiel to serve as a prophet: "Son of man, I am sending you to the children of Israel, to a rebellious nation. . . . I am sending you to them, and you shall say to them, 'Thus says the Lord GOD'" (2:3–4). God's call was not framed as an option, a suggestion, or a request. It was a command—an assignment. God commanded Ezekiel to carry out a specific role for the rest of his life, and he expected Ezekiel to obey that command. There are other individuals who received similar calls in the Old Testament, including leaders such as Saul and David, prophets such as Jeremiah and Deborah, and even artisans such as Bezalel and Aholiab (see Exodus 32). Followers of Jesus also live under a broad call to spend their lives obeying the Great Commission: "Go therefore and make disciples of all the nations, baptizing them in the name of the Father and of the Son and of the Holy Spirit, teaching them to observe all things that I have commanded you" (Matthew 28:19–20).

God equips His people to serve Him. In addition to receiving a specific call for his ministry, Ezekiel was also equipped by God with the necessary resources to carry out that call. For example, God fortified Ezekiel with the conviction necessary for dealing with the generationally stiff-necked children of Israel. More importantly, God equipped Ezekiel with His word and His Spirit: "Then the Spirit entered me when He spoke to me, and set me on my feet; and I heard Him who spoke to me" (2:2) Both chapters 2 and 3 include an extended sequence in which Ezekiel is given a scroll (representing the Word of God) and commanded to eat it: "Moreover He said to me, 'Son of man, eat what you find; eat this scroll, and go, speak to the house of Israel.' So I opened my mouth, and He caused me to eat that scroll" (3:1–2). In a similar way, as disciples of Jesus, we have been uniquely and specifically equipped to carry out our roles within God's kingdom. Like Ezekiel, that equipping includes the indwelling of God's Holy Spirit and access to God's Word through the Scriptures.

REFLECTING ON THE TEXT

5)   How do Christians encounter God's glory today?

_____

_____

_____

_____

_____

_____

_____

_____

6)   What are some of the gifts God gives to His people for service to Him? Where in the Bible are these described?

_____

_____

_____

_____

_____

_____

_____

7)   What are we risking when we ignore or reject God's specific call on our lives? What blessings come with obedience to that call?

_____

_____

_____

_____

_____

_____

_____

8) How has God equipped you with specific gifts and resources?

_____

_____

_____

_____

_____

_____

PERSONAL RESPONSE

9) How would you describe your specific calling within God's kingdom? What mission are you working to accomplish?

_____

_____

_____

_____

_____

_____

_____

10) Where do you have an opportunity right now to use your gifts and resources as tools to help carry out the Great Commission?

_____

_____

_____

_____

_____

_____

_____

2

PORTRAYING A SIEGE
Ezekiel 4:1–8:18

DRAWING NEAR
When has an illustration or object lesson helped to drive home a biblical truth for you?

_____

_____

_____

_____

_____

_____

_____

_____

_____

_____

_____

_____

_____

_____

_____

_____

_____

_____

_____

_____

_____

THE CONTEXT

We often think of the Old Testament prophets as those who spoke the word of God—which is true. But God also commanded many of His prophets to dramatize or illustrate His prophetic words in ways that were designed to catch their attention and even shock them out of complacency. One example is Jeremiah breaking a "potter's flask" in the presence of Jerusalem's leaders (see Jeremiah 19:1–14) to illustrate the disaster that would come. Another is God commanding Hosea, "Go, take yourself a wife of harlotry and children of harlotry, for the land has committed great harlotry by departing from the LORD" (Hosea 1:2).

Yet no prophet used these visual displays more frequently or more prominently than Ezekiel. We see this in the chapters of Ezekiel's prophecy that we will cover in this lesson, where the Lord instructed His prophet to draw (or scratch) a picture of Jerusalem and then act out a siege against it—including visualizing the extreme methods the residents of the city would use to cook food. God called Ezekiel to cut, weigh, and burn his own hair; to prophesy against the mountains of Jerusalem; and to relate a powerful vision of idolatry in the temple.

Importantly, chapters 4–7 in the book of Ezekiel include a series of prophecies given over the course of a year that proclaim God's judgment against Judah and Jerusalem. Ezekiel prophesied this judgment would come through the nation of Babylon. While the Babylonians had previously defeated Judah and taken many of its people captive (including Ezekiel), this coming judgment would include a devastating siege and the complete destruction of the city. Ezekiel 8 offers additional insights into the idolatry and detestable practice of Judah's spiritual leaders, which again contributed to God's judgment.

KEYS TO THE TEXT

Read Ezekiel 4:1–8:18, noting the key words and phrases indicated below.

> SIGNS OF COMING JUDGMENT: *Ezekiel's first series of prophecies, given over a year's time, describes the coming conquest of Jerusalem by the Babylonians in 586 BC.*

4:1–3. TAKE A CLAY TABLET .... PORTRAY ... JERUSALEM: Ezekiel's object lesson employed a soft tile (clay brick) to create a miniature city layout of Jerusalem with walls and siege objects that would illustrate Babylon's final coming siege of Jerusalem (588–586 BC).

4–6. LIE . . . ON YOUR LEFT SIDE . . . RIGHT SIDE: Ezekiel's act of lying on his side (likely facing north) illustrated God applying His judgment to Israel, while the prophet's act of facing south pointed to judgment on Judah. It is not necessary to assume that Ezekiel was in the prone position all the time. He was also doubtless upright part of each day, as his need for preparing food in verse 9 indicates.

4, 6. YOU SHALL BEAR THEIR INIQUITY: Ezekiel's action was not to represent the time of Israel's sinning but the time of her punishment.

5. THREE HUNDRED AND NINETY: Each day symbolized a year (see verse 6). Israel, in the north, was accountable during this span of time whose beginning and end is uncertain.

6. FORTY: Judah was also guilty, but the forty cannot represent less guilt (see Ezekiel 23:11). It may extend the time beyond the 390 days/years to 430 days/years, or they may run concurrently, but the exact duration is uncertain.

7. ARM . . . UNCOVERED: A symbol for being ready for action, as a soldier would do (see Isaiah 52:10).

8. I WILL RESTRAIN YOU: This was to symbolize the impossibility of the Jews being able to shake off their punishment.

9–13. MAKE BREAD: Scarcity of food in the eighteen-month siege especially necessitated the mixing of all kinds of grain for bread. The "twenty shekels" would be about eight ounces, while "one-sixth of a hin" would be less than a quart. There would be minimums for daily rations. It must be noted that the command of verse 12 regarding "human waste" relates only to the fuel used to prepare the food. Bread was baked on hot stones (see 1 Kings 19:6) heated by human waste because no other fuel was available. This was repulsive and polluting (see Deuteronomy 23:12–14), so the Lord calls it "defiled bread" (verse 13).

14–15. NEVER DEFILED: Ezekiel, like Daniel, had convictions to be undefiled even in his food (see Daniel 1:8). So God permitted Ezekiel to use dried cow chips as fuel for cooking his food in gracious deference to His spokesman's sensitivity (see Ezekiel 44:31).

16–17. BREAD . . . WATER: The people were soon to have neither bread nor water in any amount, and they were to grieve over the famine and their iniquity (see Leviticus 26:21–26).

5:1–4. A BARBER'S RAZOR: God's instruction for Ezekiel to shave his hair was to illustrate the severe humiliation that would come to the people of Judah at the hand of enemies, emphasizing calamities to three segments of Jerusalem due to the Babylonian conquest. Some were punished by fire (that is, pestilence and famine), others died by the enemy's sword, and some were dispersed and pursued by death (see verse 12). The small part of Ezekiel's hair that clung to his garment (see verse 3) depicted a remaining remnant, some of whom would be subject to further calamity (see verse 4; see also Ezekiel 6:8; Jeremiah 41–44).

> MESSAGES CONCERNING JUDGMENT: *Instead of being a witness to the heathen nations, Israel had exceeded them in idolatrous practices. Since the people were unique in their disobedience, they were to be outstanding in their punishment.*

5. JERUSALEM: Here, the great city alone is not meant, but is used representatively of the whole land which, despite its strategic opportunity and responsibility, rejected God.

7. YOU HAVE MULTIPLIED DISOBEDIENCE: The nations had maintained their familiar idols while Israel had defected from their true and living God. The people of Israel were worse than the pagans in proportion to spiritual knowledge and privileges and would receive God's judgment for it. The judgments of God are always relative to light and privilege granted.

8–10. I . . . WILL EXECUTE JUDGMENTS: The book of Lamentations reveals how literally these promises were realized (see 2:22; 4:10). Down through the centuries had come the threats of Leviticus 26:29 and Deuteronomy 28:53. They were taken up by Jeremiah (see 19:9; see also Isaiah 9:20) and sealed in the life of the disobedient nation. Even the remnant would be scattered and suffer.

11. AS I LIVE: Here is a solemn oath pledging the very existence of God for the fulfillment of the prophecy. This phrase is found fourteen times in this book. The people's greatest sin was defiling the sanctuary, showing the height of their wickedness.

12. PESTILENCE . . . FAMINE . . . SWORD . . . SCATTER: The four well-known judgments (see verses 2–4) of pestilence, famine, sword, and scattering were to be their judgment. They had no place to offer atoning blood, thus bearing their sins without relief.

13–15. THUS SHALL MY ANGER BE SPENT: Ezekiel's purpose was to impress on Israel's conscience God's intense hatred of idolatry and apostasy. "Fury" and "anger" are repeated six times.

16. ARROWS OF FAMINE: The evil arrows included hail, rain, mice, locusts, and mildew (see Deuteronomy 32:23–24).

17. I, THE LORD, HAVE SPOKEN: See verses 13, 15 for the same expression, which was God's personal signature on their doom.

6:3. SAYS THE LORD . . . TO THE MOUNTAINS: God had the prophet do this because the people worshiped at idol altars in the "high places" (see Leviticus 26:30–33; Isaiah 65:7; Jeremiah 3:6; Hosea 4:13; Micah 6:1–2).

4. IDOLS: This term is related to a Hebrew verb that means "to roll" (see Genesis 29:3; Joshua 10:18). It refers to shapeless things like stones or tree logs, out of which idols were made (see Ezekiel 6:9; 20:39; 22:3; 1 Kings 21:26). Ezekiel always uses this Hebrew term for idols contemptuously, as these false gods had led Israel away from their true Lord (see Ezekiel 14:5). The word may be related to a similar Hebrew expression meaning "dung pellets." Later Jewish commentators mocked these as the "dung idols"; that is, idols as worthless as dung.

7. YOU SHALL KNOW THAT I AM THE LORD: This clause recurs in verses 10, 13–14, and sixty times elsewhere in the book. It shows that the essential reason for judgment is the violation of the character of God. This is repeatedly acknowledged in Leviticus 18–26, where the motive for all obedience to God's law is the fact that He is the Lord God.

8–10. I WILL LEAVE A REMNANT: The masses of people were rejected, but grace and mercy were given to a godly remnant in the nation. There never has been, nor ever will be, a complete end to Israel. (The doctrine of the remnant can be studied in Isaiah 1:9; 10:20; Jeremiah 43:5; Zephaniah 2:7; 3:13; Zechariah 10:9; Romans 9:6–13; 11:5.)

14. DIBLAH: A reference to Diblathaim, a city on the eastern edge of Moab (see Numbers 33:46; Jeremiah 48:22), near the desert, east and south of the Dead Sea.

THE END HAS COME: *The lament that follows in this chapter declares the land of Israel was ripe for judgment. God's patience has ended.*

7:1–9. DOOM HAS COME TO YOU: The final destruction of Jerusalem by Nebuchadnezzar is in view (586 BC).

10. THE ROD HAS BLOSSOMED: Ezekiel explains this in verse 11. Violence had grown up into a rod of wickedness, which likely refers to Nebuchadnezzar, the instrument of God's vengeance (see Isaiah 10:5; Jeremiah 51:20).

PRIDE HAS BUDDED: Pride comes when humans think they can live without God. However, this godlessness only leads to shame and ultimate destruction (see Proverbs 11:2; 13:10; Jeremiah 49:16; see also Ezekiel 16:56; 30:6).

12. BUYER REJOICE . . . SELLER MOURN: Such matters of business were meaningless because the Chaldeans (Babylonians) took all the land and killed those they didn't take captive (verse 15), while the rest escaped (verse 16). Wealth was useless (verses 19–20).

13. SELLER SHALL NOT RETURN TO . . . SOLD: There was to be no Jubilee year, in which all lands were returned to their original owners (see Leviticus 25).

17–22. EVERY HAND WILL BE FEEBLE: This section describes the mourning of the helpless and frightened people. In distress, they recognized the uselessness of the things in which they trusted. Their wealth provided nothing. Their "silver and gold" (verse 19) and their "ornaments" (verse 20) were as useless as the idols they made with them.

22. MY SECRET PLACE: The Holy of Holies in the temple, that place where the high priest could only enter once a year to make atonement in God's presence, will be desecrated by pagans.

23. MAKE A CHAIN: Ezekiel is to perform another emblematic act of captivity (see Jeremiah 27:2; Nahum 3:10).

24. THE WORST OF THE GENTILES: Babylonian pagans.

27. ACCORDING TO WHAT THEY DESERVE: See Genesis 18:25.

VISIONS CONCERNING ABOMINATION: *This portion of Ezekiel's prophecy deals with details that God conveyed to him only in visions. The prophet's trip to Jerusalem was in spirit only, while his body physically remained in his house.*

8:1. THE SIXTH YEAR: This occurred during 592 BC (see Ezekiel 1:2) in August/September, a year and two months after the first vision (1:1).

THE HAND OF THE LORD: This ushered the prophet into a series of visions (see verse 3) stretching to the end of Ezekiel 11.

2. A LIKENESS: The prophet saw God's glory (see verse 4), as in 1:26–28.

3. IN VISIONS OF GOD: In visions, Ezekiel went to the city of Jerusalem; and in visions, he returned to Babylon (see 11:24). After God finished the visions, Ezekiel told his home audience what he had seen. The visions are not a description of deeds done in the past in Israel but a survey of Israel's current condition as they existed at that very time.

THE SEAT . . . IMAGE OF JEALOUSY: God represents to Ezekiel the image of an idol (see Deuteronomy 4:16) in the entrance to the inner court of the temple.

It is called "the image of jealousy" because it provoked the Lord to jealousy (see Ezekiel 5:13; 16:38; 36:6; 38:19; Exodus 20:5).

4. THE GLORY OF . . . GOD: God was also there in glory, but He was ignored while the people worshiped the idol (verse 6).

6. TO MAKE ME GO FAR AWAY: Sin would expel the people from their land and God from His sanctuary.

7–12. THERE WAS A HOLE IN THE WALL: This section describes "greater abominations" (verse 6) of idolatry; namely, a secret cult of idolatrous elders.

8. DIG INTO THE WALL . . . A DOOR: This indicates the clandestine (see verse 12) secrecy of these idolaters, practicing their cult in hiding.

10. PORTRAYED . . . ON THE WALLS: The temple's walls are ugly, with graffiti featuring creatures linked with Egyptian animal cults (see Romans 1:23) and other idols. Leaders of Israel, who should be worshiping the God of the temple, were offering incense to them.

11. SEVENTY . . . ELDERS: Obviously, this was not the Sanhedrin, since that was not formed until after the restoration from Babylon, though the pattern had been suggested much earlier (see Exodus 24:9–10; Numbers 11:16). These men were appointed to guard against idolatry.

JAAZANIAH . . . SON OF SHAPHAN: If he was the son of the Shaphan who read God's Word to Josiah (2 Kings 22:8–11), we have some concept of the depth of sin to which the leaders had fallen. He is not to be confused with the man in Ezekiel 11:1, who had a different father.

14. WEEPING FOR TAMMUZ: A greater abomination than the secret cult involved Israel's worship of the Babylonian deity Tammuz or Dumuzi (Duzu), beloved of Ishtar, the god of spring vegetation. Vegetation burned in the summer, died in the winter, and came to life in the spring. The women mourned over the god's demise in July and longed for his revival. The fourth month of the Hebrew calendar still bears the name Tammuz. The basest immoralities were connected with the worship of this idol.

16. WORSHIPING THE SUN: In the most sacred inner court, where only priests could go, was the crowning insult to God. Twenty-five men were worshiping the sun as an idol (see Deuteronomy 4:19; 2 Kings 23:5, 11; Job 31:26; Jeremiah 44:17). These twenty-five represent the twenty-four orders of priests plus the high priest.

17. PUT THE BRANCH TO THEIR NOSE: The meaning is uncertain, but it seems to have been some act of contempt toward God. The Septuagint translators rendered it, "they are as mockers."

18. I . . . WILL ACT IN FURY: God must judge intensely due to such horrible sins (see Ezekiel 24:9–10).

UNLEASHING THE TEXT

1) What do you find most surprising about Ezekiel's visual displays in 4:1–17? Why?

_____

_____

_____

_____

_____

_____

2) Try to place yourself among the exiles of Ezekiel's day. How would you respond if you regularly encountered a prophet demonstrating a siege against a city, cooking meager food over dung, shaving off his own hair, and so on? Why did this moment call for such displays?

_____

_____

_____

_____

_____

_____

_____

3) What promises did God make in Ezekiel 5:15–17? What was the purpose of those promises?

_____

_____

_____

_____

_____

_____

4) What do you learn about God's character from Ezekiel 7:1–27?

_____

_____

_____

_____

_____

_____

_____

EXPLORING THE MEANING

Sin always carries consequences. God specifically instructed Ezekiel to act out the future siege of Jerusalem (and complete conquest of Judah) by the Babylonians. The primary goal of these acts was to display the devastating consequences of sin. By lying on his side for 430 days, Ezekiel bore the iniquity of Israel's sin and Judah's sin, respectively. The weight of that reality pressed down on the prophet day after day, immobilizing him. Similarly, God's instructions for Ezekiel to eat meager rations of food and cook them over human dung—which was later modified to cow dung—revealed the terrible circumstances the people of Jerusalem would experience during the actual siege. Imagine the reaction of Ezekiel's fellow captives as they watched him physically waste away day after day from near starvation! This illustration—this picture—revealed the serious consequences of Judah's rebellion against God over a period of centuries. The same reality holds true today. We reject God and choose to sin because we think it will bring us pleasure or power or prestige, but in reality, sin only produces pain.

All sin is a form of idolatry. The nation of Israel had been uniquely blessed and gifted with the revelation of God. They had been chosen for the specific purpose of revealing God to the rest of the world. Yet, for centuries, God's chosen people had ignored the reality of their calling and even rejected it. Rather than being a witness of God to the nations, they had turned to the religious practices of those nations. God's words in Ezekiel 5:7–8 are sobering: "Because you have multiplied disobedience more than the nations that are all around you. . . . Indeed I, even I, am against you and will execute judgments in your midst in the sight of the nations." Israel had rejected the true God and turned to false gods, which is idolatry. Similarly, all sin is rooted in idolatry. Even today, our sin is rooted in idolatry. Every time we turn away from God to serve something else—including our own desires or our own purposes—we are elevating that something else above God. We are practicing idolatry.

Even in the face of idolatry, God remains merciful. Sin and idolatry always carry lasting consequences in our lives. God's judgment against Jerusalem (and, more broadly, against the nation of Israel) is an example of that reality. At the same time, God's dealings with His people also reflect His mercy and grace. In Ezekiel 5, we read how God told His prophet to shave his hair and beard as a representation of Israel. One-third of the hair was burned, one-third struck with the sword, and one-third scattered to the winds (exile). Yet God also commanded Ezekiel to "take a small number of them and bind them in the edge of your garment" (verse 3). God would later explain this picture in chapter 6: "Yet I will leave a remnant, so that you may have some who escape the sword among the nations, when you are scattered through the countries. Then those of you who escape will remember Me among the nations where they are carried captive" (verses 8–9). Because of His grace, God has never allowed Israel to be fully destroyed. He has remained faithful to His people in spite of their continued rejection of Him.

REFLECTING ON THE TEXT

5) In what ways do you see our culture experiencing the consequences of sin?

_____

_____

_____

_____

_____

6) What are some examples of idolatry that are actually affirmed and *celebrated* within our culture? What about within the church?

_____

_____

_____

_____

_____

_____

7) How would you describe the connection between idolatry and all other forms of sin?

_____

_____

_____

_____

_____

_____

_____

_____

8) The Bible reveals God is both holy and merciful—a God of wrath and of grace. How are those two aspects of God's character displayed through the gospel?

_____

_____

_____

_____

_____

_____

PERSONAL RESPONSE

9) When have you experienced the mercy of God in a way that was especially noteworthy to you?

_____

_____

_____

_____

_____

_____

_____

_____

10) Where are you currently in danger of idolatry—of placing something or someone ahead of God in terms of your affection, adoration, or worship?

_____

_____

_____

_____

_____

_____

_____

_____

_____

_____

_____

_____

3

GOD'S GLORY DEPARTS
Ezekiel 9:1–13:23

DRAWING NEAR

What are some of the biggest changes or cultural shifts you have experienced over the course of your life? How have those shifts impacted your life?

_____

_____

_____

_____

_____

_____

_____

_____

_____

_____

_____

_____

_____

_____

_____

_____

_____

_____

_____

_____

_____

THE CONTEXT

As we discussed in the previous lesson, for eighteen months the Lord had used Ezekiel as a visual display of His coming judgment against Jerusalem and the nation of Israel. During that time, Ezekiel verbally declared the specifics of that judgment through several prophecies (recorded in 5:5–7:27). Ezekiel 8 marks a turning point in the book. The prophet was lifted by the Holy Spirit "between earth and heaven" (verse 3) and given a series of visions regarding the idolatry being practiced in Jerusalem, including the detestable rituals of its leaders.

These visions continue into chapters 9–11, which we will explore in more depth in this lesson. They include heavenly angels called to carry out God's judgment against the city—though several members of the community are marked as faithful and promised protection. The visions also include the striking departure of God's glory from the temple, which occurs in several stages. Chapter 11 reveals a collection of twenty-five leaders giving deceptive advice to God's people and another promise of future restoration once God's judgment is complete.

Chapter 12 marks another turning point in the book of Ezekiel. For several chapters (12:1–24:27), the prophet will turn his attention to his fellow captives living in Babylon. Much like the residents of Judah, these captives were hard-hearted and refused to believe that Jerusalem would be destroyed. They believed they would return soon to their homes—and to the protection of the Lord—in spite of their continued rejection of His will. God used Ezekiel to explain the error of their thinking and the many reasons for the climax of judgment that would soon fall on Judah and Jerusalem.

KEYS TO THE TEXT

Read Ezekiel 9:1–13:23, noting the key words and phrases indicated below.

> GOD'S GLORY BEGINS TO LIFT: *Ezekiel continues to relate his vision, now describing how God's glory began to depart from the temple in Jerusalem.*

9:1. CHARGE OVER THE CITY: God here summons His servant angels to carry out His judgments. These angelic executioners (see Daniel 4:13, 17, 23) came equipped with weapons of destruction.

2. SIX MEN: Angels can appear like men when they are ministering on the earth (see Genesis 18:1; Daniel 9:20–23).

ONE MAN: He was superior to the others. Linen indicates high rank (see Daniel 10:5; 12:6). Perhaps this was the Angel of the Lord, the preincarnate Christ. He had all the instruments of an oriental scribe to carry out His task (see Ezekiel 9:4, 11).

3. THE GLORY . . . HAD GONE UP: The glory of God departs before the destruction of the city and temple. The gradual departure of God from His temple is depicted in stages: the glory resides in the temple's Most Holy Place, between the wings of the cherubs on each side of the ark of the covenant over the mercy seat. It then leaves to the front door (see verse 3; 10:4), later to the east gate by the outer wall (see 10:18–19), and finally to the Mount of Olives to the east, having fully departed (see 11:22–23). The glory will return in the future kingdom of the Messiah (see 43:2–7).

4. PUT A MARK ON THE FOREHEADS OF THE MEN: Since God's departure removed all protection and gave the people over to destruction, it was necessary for the angelic scribe (the Angel of the Lord) to mark for God's preservation the righteous who had been faithful to Him, not unlike blood on the lintel to protect Israel from the Lord's judgment in Egypt (see Exodus 12:21–30). Those left unmarked were subject to death in Babylon's siege (see Ezekiel 9:5). The mark was the indication of God's elect, identified personally by the preincarnate Christ. He was marking the elect (see Exodus 12:7). Malachi 3:16–18 indicates a similar idea (see also Revelation 7:3; 9:4). The marked ones were penitent and thus identified for protection. Here was a respite of grace for the remnant. The rest were to be killed (see Ezekiel 9:5–7).

8–11. WILL YOU DESTROY ALL THE REMNANT OF ISRAEL: Ezekiel is fearfully aroused in prayer because the judgment on Jerusalem and Israel is so vast. God replies (verses 9–10) that pervasive sin demands thorough judgment, yet comforts him by the report that the faithful had been marked to be spared (verse 11). (See Romans 11:1–2, 25–27.)

10:1 THE LIKENESS OF A THRONE: The glory of God rises above the angelic servants, the same four as in Ezekiel 1 (see also 10:20, 22), and also above the throne described in 1:26–28 on which God sits (see also 10:20). From there, God directs the operation of His war machine ("wheels"; see notes on 1:15–16) on Jerusalem (see 10:2). The throne is like a sapphire shining forth, representing the Lord's glory and holiness (see 11:22).

2. FILL . . . WITH COALS: God specifies that the marking angel (see 9:2, 11) should reach into the war machine and fill his hands with fiery coals in the

presence of the angels of chapter 1. These coals picture the fires of judgment which God's angels are to "scatter" on Jerusalem. In Isaiah 6, "coals" were used for the purification of the prophet; here, they are used for the destruction of the wicked (see Hebrews 12:29). Fire did destroy Jerusalem in 586 BC.

3. CHERUBIM: These are different from the cherubim of Ezekiel 1 and the cherub of verse 4.

4. FILLED WITH THE CLOUD: This verse explains how the "cloud" of verse 3 "filled the inner court." It repeats what is first described in Ezekiel 9:3.

6–7. THE MAN CLOTHED IN LINEN: These verses pick up the action of the angelic scribe from verse 2.

7. CHERUB . . . PUT IT INTO THE HANDS: One of the four cherubim (of 1:5ff. and 10:1) puts the fiery coals into the marking angel's hand.

9–17. WHEELS BY THE CHERUBIM: This whole section is similar to Ezekiel 1:4–21. Four wheels on God's chariot mingled with the four angels (see 1:15–21) were coordinated with each other in precision, and each with a different one of the cherubim. All looked so much alike that it was as if one wheel blended entirely with another (10:10). As their appearance was so unified, their action was in unison and instant (verse 11). The cherubim had bodies like men and their chariot wheels were full of eyes, denoting full perception to see the sinners and their fitting judgment. The color beryl is often a sparkling yellow or gold.

14. THE FACE OF A CHERUB: This description of one of the cherubs in 1:10 indicates this was the face of an ox.

15. LIFTED UP: The cherubim were all ready to move in unison (see verses 16–17) as the Shekinah glory of God departed (see verse 18).

18–19. GLORY . . . DEPARTED: God's glory leaves to the east gate of the temple by the outer wall. There was thus written over the entire structure, as well as Israel's spiritual life, "Ichabod," meaning, "the glory has departed" (see 1 Samuel 4:21; 10:18–19).

JUDGMENT ON WICKED COUNSELORS: Ezekiel is taken in spirit to the very place where the glory of God had left and is given a vision of twenty-five men who represent influential leaders among the people who gave fatal advice to them.

11:1. BROUGHT ME TO THE EAST GATE: Ezekiel, though at the temple only in the vision (see 8:3), saw because the Lord God—who was everywhere present and all-knowing—impressed specific details on him in the vision. Here he sees twenty-five wicked leaders of the people, who are each part of God's reason for the judgment (see verses 8, 10).

JAAZANIAH THE SON OF AZZUR: See note on Ezekiel 8:11.

3. CALDRON . . . MEAT: Although this is obscure, it may be that the bad advice these leaders were giving was that the people should not be engaged in business as usual, "building houses" or taking care of their comfort and futures, when they were about to be cooked like meat in a pot over a blazing fire. The idea must have been that the people should get ready for battle and be prepared to fight, not focusing on comfort but survival. Jeremiah had told the people to surrender to the Babylonians and save their lives rather than fight and be killed (see Jeremiah 27:9–17). These false leaders, like the prophets and priests whom Jeremiah confronted for telling the people not to submit, scorned Jeremiah's words from God and would pay for it (see Ezekiel 11:4, see also 24:1–14).

6. MULTIPLIED YOUR SLAIN: The leaders who misled Israel by inciting false expectations of a victorious defense, rather than peaceful surrender, were responsible for the deadly results. Many people died in resisting Babylon.

7. I SHALL BRING YOU OUT: The false leaders thought that unless they fought, they would all be in a caldron; that is, the city. But here, the Lord promised that some would be delivered from the city, only to die on Israel's border in the wilderness (see verses 8–11). This was literally fulfilled at Riblah (see 2 Kings 25:18–21; Jeremiah 52:24–27).

13. PELATIAH . . . DIED: The death of one leader from verse 1 was a sign that God would indeed carry out His word. Apparently, this leader did die suddenly at the time Ezekiel was shown the vision, so that the prophet feared this death meant death for all Israelites (see Ezekiel 9:8).

14–15. YOUR BRETHREN: Ezekiel was told he had a new family, not the priests at Jerusalem to whom he was tied by blood, but his fellow exiles in Babylon, identified as those who were treated as outcasts. The priesthood was about to be ended, and he was to have a new family.

15. GET FAR AWAY: The contemptuous words of those still left in Jerusalem at the carrying away of Jeconiah and the exiles indicated that they felt smugly secure and believed the land was their possession.

16. LITTLE SANCTUARY: This is better rendered "for a little while"; that is, for however long the captivity lasted. God was to be the protection and provision for those who had been scattered through all the seventy years until they

were restored. The exiles may have cast off the Jews, but God had not (see Isaiah 8:14). This holds true for the future restoration of the Jews as well (see Ezekiel 11:17–18).

19–20. A NEW SPIRIT WITHIN THEM: God pledged not only to restore Ezekiel's people to their ancient land but also to bring the New Covenant with its blessings. In contrast to the Mosaic covenant under which Israel had failed, the New Covenant would have a spiritual, divine dynamic by which those who know God would participate in the blessings of salvation. The fulfillment would be to individuals, yet also to Israel as a nation (see Romans 11:16–27). In principle, this covenant, also announced by Jesus Christ (see Luke 22:20), began to be fulfilled spiritually by Jewish and Gentile believers in the church era (see 1 Corinthians 11:25; 2 Corinthians 3:6; Hebrews 8:7–13; 9:15; 10:14–17; 12:24; 13:20). It has already begun to take effect with "the remnant according to the election of grace" (Romans 11:5). It will be also realized by the people of Israel in the last days, including the regathering to their ancient land, Palestine (see Jeremiah 30–33). The streams of the Abrahamic, Davidic, and New Covenants all find their confluence in the millennial kingdom ruled by the Messiah (see Ezekiel 36:25–28; Jeremiah 31:31–34).

23. THE MOUNTAIN ... EAST: The glory of God moves to the Mount of Olives, where the glorious Son of God will return at the Second Advent (see Ezekiel 43:1–5; Zechariah 14:4).

24. BROUGHT ME IN A VISION: Again, Ezekiel has physically remained in his Babylonian house, seen by his visitors (see verse 25; 8:1). God, who supernaturally showed him a vision in Jerusalem, caused his sense of awareness to return to Chaldea, thus ending the vision state. Once the vision was completed, Ezekiel was able to tell his exiled countrymen what God had shown him (see verse 25).

> JUDAH'S CAPTIVITY PORTRAYED: *God now instructs Ezekiel to take part in another object lesson to reveal to the people of Judah what their captivity will be like.*

12:2. A REBELLIOUS HOUSE: Ezekiel's message was addressed to his fellow exiles who were as hardened as those still in Jerusalem. They were so intent on a quick return to Jerusalem that they would not accept his message of the city's destruction. Their rebellion is described in familiar terms (see Deuteronomy 29:1–4; Isaiah 6:9–10; Jeremiah 5:21; see Matthew 13:13–15; Acts 28:26–27).

3. PREPARE . . . FOR CAPTIVITY: This dramatic object lesson by the prophet called for carrying belongings out in a stealthy way as an act that depicted baggage for exile; that is, just the bare necessities. Ezekiel's fellow countrymen would carry out such baggage when they went into captivity or sought to escape during Babylon's takeover of Jerusalem (see Ezekiel 12:7, 11). Some of the people who were attempting to escape were caught as in a net, like King Zedekiah who was overtaken, blinded, and forced into exile (see verses 12–13; 2 Kings 24:18–25:7; Jeremiah 39:4–7; Ezekiel 52:1–11). Verse 7 indicates that Ezekiel actually did what he was told.

5. DIG THROUGH THE WALL: This section depicts those in desperation trying to escape from their sun-dried brick homes.

6. COVER YOUR FACE: This was to avoid recognition.

10–13. THE PRINCE: This is a reference to King Zedekiah, whom Ezekiel always referred to as a prince and never a king. Jehoiachin was regarded as the true king (see 17:13), because the Babylonians never deposed him formally. All the house of Israel, however, would share in the calamity to fall on Zedekiah. How literally these prophecies were fulfilled can be seen from the account in 2 Kings 25:1–7. The "net" and "snare" (verse 13) were the Babylonian army. Zedekiah was taken captive to Babylon, but he never saw it because his eyes had been put out at Riblah.

14–16. I WILL DRAW OUT THE SWORD . . . I WILL SPARE A FEW: God's hand would use the enemy as His rod of correction, and only a few would be left.

22. THIS PROVERB: Delay had given the people the false impression that the stroke of judgment would never come. In fact, a proverbial saying about this had become popular, no doubt developed by false prophets who caused the people to reject Ezekiel's visions and prophecies (see verse 27) and gave "false divinations" (verses 23–24) in their place.

25. IN YOUR DAYS: The prophet is explicit about the present time for fulfillment; that is, in their lifetime.

13:2. AGAINST THE PROPHETS: False prophets had long flourished in Judah and had been transported to Babylon as well. In verses 1–16, God directs Ezekiel to indict those false prophets for futile assurances of peace (as in Jeremiah 23). Then, in verses 17–23, God's attention turns to lying prophetesses. The test of a prophet is found in Deuteronomy 13:1–5 and 18:21–22.

2–3. HEART . . . SPIRIT: Spurious spokesmen prophesy subjectively while claiming to have revelation and authority from the Lord (see verse 7).

4. LIKE FOXES: THE false prophets did not do anything helpful. Rather, like foxes, they were mischievous and destructive.

5. TO BUILD A WALL: The false prophets did nothing to shore up the spiritual defenses that the people so needed in the face of judgment. The enemy had made "gaps," but the false prophets never encouraged the people to repent and return to the Lord. Those prophets who would encourage the people to repent were called for in Ezekiel 22:30.

DAY OF THE LORD: The Day of the Lord for Judah came in 586 BC when the theocracy fell. The phrase "Day of the Lord" appears nineteen times in the Old Testament and four times in the New Testament to express the time of God's extreme wrath. It can refer to a near-future judgment or a far-future judgment. At times, the near fulfillment prefigures the far fulfillment (see Joel 1:15; 3:14); on other occasions, both kinds are included in one passage (see Zephaniah 1:7, 14).

9. MY HAND WILL BE AGAINST THE PROPHETS: A threefold judgment is given to the false prophets: (1) they would not be in the council of God's people; (2) their names would be wiped from the register of Israel (see Ezra 2:62); and (3) they would never return to the land (see Ezekiel 20:38).

10–11. BUILDS A WALL: False prophets had lulled the people into a false sense of security. Phony peace promises, while sin continued on the brink of God's judgment, was a way of erecting a defective wall and whitewashing it to make it look good. Such an unsafe wall was doomed to collapse when God would bring His storm, picturing the invaders' assault (see verse 11).

11–16. FLOODING RAIN . . . HAILSTONES . . . STORMY WIND: These descriptions are all images belonging to the illustration of the wall, not meant to convey real wind, flood, and hail. The Babylonians were the actual destroyers of Israel's hypocritical, false spirituality.

17–23. DAUGHTERS OF YOUR PEOPLE, WHO PROPHESY: Although women were rebuked by the prophet Isaiah (see 3:16–4:1; 32:9–13) and by the prophet Amos (see 4:1–3), this is the only Old Testament text where false prophetesses are mentioned. Sorcery was practiced mainly by women. Jezebel is called a false prophetess in Revelation 2:20.

18–19. CHARMS . . . VEILS . . . HANDFULS OF BARLEY . . . BREAD: Apparently, these sorceresses employed all these items in their divinations, hunting down people for their advantage (see Ezekiel 13:20).

22. WITH LIES: Predators had saddened the righteous through their false message, leading to calamity that involved great loss even for them (see 21:3–4).

They had encouraged the wicked to expect a bright future and saw no need to repent to avoid death.

23. I WILL DELIVER MY PEOPLE: Certainly, this was true in the restoration after the seventy years in Babylon, but it will be fully true in the Messiah's kingdom. God's true promise will bring an end to sorcery and false prophecy (see Micah 3:6–7; Zechariah 13:1–6).

UNLEASHING THE TEXT

1) What emotions did Ezekiel express throughout chapter 9? How did these emotions relate to the surrounding events?

_____

_____

_____

_____

_____

_____

_____

2) Chapter 10 reveals another manifestation of God's glory. How does that manifestation differ from what Ezekiel recorded in chapters 1 and 2?

_____

_____

_____

_____

_____

_____

3) How would you summarize the object lessons Ezekiel carried out in chapter 12? What was their purpose among the captives in Babylon?

_____

_____

_____

_____

_____

_____

4) What was Ezekiel's message to the false prophets, as recorded in chapter 13?

_____

_____

_____

_____

_____

_____

EXPLORING THE MEANING

God knows those who belong to Him. Ezekiel 9 offers a "behind the scenes" view of the spiritual realm. While physically "seeing" Jerusalem in a vision, Ezekiel also witnessed six angelic beings charged with carrying out God's judgment against the city. Appearing as men, these angels each carried "a deadly weapon in his hand" (verse 1). One of the angels was given the task of identifying individuals in the city who still feared God. He was commanded to "mark" the foreheads of those who wept over the evil done there. The rest of the angels were given a chilling command: "Go after him through the city and kill; do not let your eye spare, nor have any pity. Utterly slay old and young men, maidens and little children and women; but do not come near anyone on whom is the mark" (verses 5–6). God's judgment against evil is always frightening, but the larger implication of this vision is encouraging for God's people—namely, He knows those who are His own. Even when we live within a wicked and corrupt culture, our Savior cares about and is faithful toward those who remain faithful to Him.

God separates Himself from sin. About 300 years before Ezekiel's prophetic ministry, King Solomon supervised the construction of a magnificent temple in Jerusalem. This temple was built as God's house—a place for His name to dwell in the midst of His people. During the dedication of that temple, "fire came down from heaven and consumed the burnt offering and the sacrifices; and the glory of the LORD filled the temple. And the priests could not enter the house of the LORD, because the glory of the LORD had filled the LORD's house" (2 Chronicles 7:1–2). God manifested Himself within the temple to confirm His presence in the community of Israel. This is why Ezekiel's vision in chapters 9–11 is so striking: the prophet witnessed a similar manifestation of God's glory, but in reverse. The glory of the Lord moved from the cherubim in the Holy of Holies, out to the threshold of the temple (see Ezekiel 9:3), then departed from the threshold (see 10:18), and then "the glory of the LORD went up from the midst of the city and stood on the mountain, which is on the east side of the city" (11:23). God removed His presence from the temple and from the community of Israel because of continued sin.

God's kingdom will be fully established. The unified message of Ezekiel and other prophets of his day was that Israel's repeated rebellion had finally resulted in God removing His presence from the community. However, Ezekiel and other Old Testament prophets also made it clear this separation was temporary. At a coming day in the future, God would reestablish His kingdom on earth in a physical and even geopolitical way. This is often referred to as the millennial kingdom—1,000 years of peace on earth when Christ, the Messiah, will reign in Jerusalem as King of kings and Lord of lords (see Revelation 20:1–6). Ezekiel offered many prophecies about this coming time period. In chapter 11, specifically, he described the spiritual renewal that will take place in Israel during that future kingdom: "Then I will give them one heart, and I will put a new spirit within them, and take the stony heart out of their flesh, and give them a heart of flesh, that they may walk in My statutes and keep My judgments and do them; and they shall be My people, and I will be their God" (verses 19–20).

REFLECTING ON THE TEXT

5) Is it good news or bad news that God knows the condition of our hearts as individuals? Explain your answer.

_____

_____

_____

_____

_____

6) How does God manifest Himself to the world today?

_____

_____

_____

_____

7) When have you felt a separation from God because of sin? What is the right response to that feeling?

_____

_____

_____

_____

8) Describe the spiritual renewal that Scripture foretells will take place in Israel during the Millennium. What did God promise to do for His people?

_____

_____

_____

PERSONAL RESPONSE

9) Are there any areas of your life that you are trying to hide from God? Why do people try to hide from God, even though they know it is impossible?

_____

_____

_____

_____

_____

10) What is one specific step that you will take this week to draw closer to God?

_____

_____

_____

_____

_____

_____

4

JUDGMENT ON IDOLATRY
Ezekiel 14:1–17:24

DRAWING NEAR

What do you think of when you think of an idol? Are the idols of your context statues and shrines, or idols of the heart?

_____

_____

_____

_____

_____

_____

_____

_____

_____

_____

_____

_____

_____

_____

_____

_____

_____

_____

_____

_____

_____

THE CONTEXT

As we have seen, Ezekiel 12–24 makes up an extended prophetic record that Ezekiel directed primarily toward his fellow captives who were living in Babylon. These captives were largely made up of those who had been wealthy and/ or educated in the community of Judah, including commercial, political, and religious leaders. In other words, many of these captives had helped steer Judah in the wrong direction. Given this, it is not surprising that they still failed to grasp the reality of their situation while in captivity. Many of Ezekiel's contemporaries believed that their captivity would be short-lived—that God would "fix" things and return them to Jerusalem.

As we will explore in this lesson, Ezekiel made every effort to show them the error in their thinking. In chapter 14, he confronts a group of "elders of Israel" (verse 1) who were among the captives, revealing their idolatry. In chapter 15, he offers an object lesson of Israel as a useless vine, fit only to be burned as fuel in a fire. In chapter 16, he paints a picture of God's deep and personal love for Israel as a nation—and of Israel's deep personal betrayal by pursuing the gods of other nations. In chapter 17, he uses another illustration (this time of an eagle) to describe God's faithfulness and Israel's unfaithfulness in their recent history.

Throughout each of these visions, prophecies, and separate methods of communication, God's goal through Ezekiel was the same. He wanted to confront the captives with the reality of their sin and need to repent. Again and again, God emphasized His faithfulness to His people alongside the reality of His imminent judgment because of Israel's unfaithfulness.

KEYS TO THE TEXT

Read Ezekiel 14:1–17:24, noting the key words and phrases indicated below.

> *IDOLS IN THEIR HEARTS: Elders from Israel come to Ezekiel pretending to seek God's counsel. The Lord sees through their façade and indicts them for determining to pursue their own evil ways and continue to defy His will.*

14:1–3. NOW SOME OF THE ELDERS OF ISRAEL CAME: False prophets, like the ones whom Ezekiel identifies in chapter 13, were thriving in Israel, as the civil leaders and populace whom they represented set a welcoming climate and inclination for the delusions.

4. I THE LORD WILL ANSWER: The elders received no verbal answer but rather a message directly from the Lord in the form of judgment.

6. TURN AWAY: The Lord answered the two-faced inquiry in only one way: by a call to repent. The seekers were turned away from Him to idols (verse 6b), and He must be turned away from them (verse 8a). The guilty, including those back at Jerusalem and the exiles tolerating the same things, were to repent by turning away from idols to God.

8. SET MY FACE AGAINST: The punishment from God echoed the warnings of Leviticus 20:3, 5–6 and Deuteronomy 28:27.

9. THE PROPHET IS INDUCED: God will deceive a false prophet only in a qualified sense. When one willfully rejects His Word, He places a resulting cloud of darkness, or permits it to continue, hiding the truth so that the person is deceived by his own obstinate self-will. This fits with the same principle as when God gives up Israel to evil statutes (see Ezekiel 20:25–26), counsel that they insist on following as they spurn His Word (see 20:24, 26). When people refuse the truth, God lets them seek after their own inclinations and gives them over to falsehood (see 20:39). This is the wrath of abandonment that Paul noted in Romans 1:18–32 (see also 1 Kings 22:20–23; 2 Thessalonians 2:11).

12. THE WORD OF THE LORD CAME AGAIN TO ME: Ezekiel here answered a deceptive teaching that God would never judge the people of Judah, since some righteous people were among them. God would honor the presence of the godly (see verses 14, 20).

13–20. MY HAND AGAINST: God promises four acts in His drama of judgment: (1) famine, (2) ravages by wild beasts, (3) the sword, and (4) pestilence.

14–20. EVEN IF . . . NOAH, DANIEL, AND JOB: Jeremiah 7:16 and 15:1–4 provide a close parallel to this passage. According to Jeremiah, even Moses and Samuel, well known for their power in intercessory prayer, would not prevail to deliver Jerusalem and the people. The three Old Testament heroes mentioned in this section in Ezekiel exhibited the power of intercession on behalf of others (see Genesis 6:18; Job 42:7–10; Daniel 1; 2) at strategic points in redemptive history, but even they could not deliver anyone but themselves. Even the presence and prayers of the godly could not stop the coming judgment. Genesis 18:22–32 and Jeremiah 5:1–4 provide rare exceptions to the principle that one person's righteousness is no protection for others.

22–23. THEIR WAYS AND THEIR DOINGS: An ungodly Jerusalem remnant, brought as captives to join the exiled Jews in Babylon, were to be very wicked.

Exiles already there, repulsed by this evil, were to realize God's justness in His severe judgment on Jerusalem.

15:1–3. THEN THE WORD . . . CAME: Israel, often symbolized by a vine (see Ezekiel 17:6–10; Genesis 49:22; Jeremiah 2:21), had become useless. Failing to do the very thing God set her apart to do—bear fruit—she no longer served any purpose and was useless (verse 2). Other trees can be used for construction of certain things, but a fruitless vine is useless (verse 3), having no value. In every age, the people of God have their value in their fruitfulness.

4–5. THROWN INTO THE FIRE: The burning of the fruitless vine symbolized judgment in the deportations of 605 BC and 597 BC, leading up to the final conquest in 586 BC. Isaiah made the same analogy in his prophecy (see Isaiah 5:1–7), saying that Israel produced only useless, sour berries.

6–8. THEREFORE: The prophet applies the symbol to Israel and predicts the desolation of the city and the land. In the time of the Great Tribulation, it will be so again (see Revelation 14:18).

> GOD'S LOVE FOR HIS PEOPLE: *In this section, the story of Israel's unfaithfulness to the love of God is told in all its sordid, vile character. The chapter is so sad and indicting that some of the ancient rabbis did not allow it to be read in public.*

16:1. THE WORD: This chapter, the longest one in Ezekiel, is similar to chapter 23 in that both indict Judah as spiritually immoral (see verse 2). The opening section (verses 1–7) covers the period from Abraham entering Canaan (Genesis 12) through the exile in Egypt (Exodus 12).

3–5. YOUR BIRTH: Israel was like an abandoned child. In verses 4–14, God recounts the history of Israel from her conception to her glory under Solomon.

3. AMORITE . . . HITTITE: These names identify the residents of Canaan who occupied the land when Abraham migrated there (see Genesis 12:5–6). Jerusalem had the same moral character as the rest of Canaan (see also Ezekiel 16:45).

4–5. NO EYE PITIED YOU: Israel, in the day of her birth, was unwanted and uncared for.

6. WHEN I PASSED BY YOU: The time intended here is probably the patriarchal period of Abraham, Isaac, and Jacob, when God formed His people.

7. THRIVE: This refers more to the people than to the land. It seems to refer to the time of Israel's growth during the 430-year stay in Egypt; wild but flourish-

ing and beautiful, Israel was "naked," without the benefits of culture and civilization (see Exodus 1:7, 9, 12).

8–14. WHEN I PASSED BY YOU AGAIN: This is best taken as the time from the Exodus (Exodus 12ff.) through David's reign (1 Kings 2).

8. THE TIME OF LOVE: This refers to the marriageable state. A man spreading his "wing" was a custom of espousal (see Ruth 3:9) and here indicates that God had entered into a covenant with the young nation at Mount Sinai (see Exodus 19:5–8). Making a covenant pictures marriage, the figure of God's relation to Israel (see Jeremiah 2:2; 3:1ff.; Hosea 2:2–23).

9–14. I CLOTHED YOU: The gifts mentioned in this section were customarily marriage gifts presented to a queen. The crowning may refer to the reigns of David and Solomon, when Jerusalem became the royal city. Israel was actually a small kingdom but with a great reputation (see 1 Kings 10). This refers to the time from Joshua's conquest of Canaan (Joshua 3ff.) through David's reign (1 Kings 2) and into Solomon's time (before 1 Kings 11).

14. MY SPLENDOR: The nation was truly a trophy of God's grace (see Deuteronomy 7:6–8). The presence and glory of the Lord provided Jerusalem with her beauty and prominence.

15–19. YOU . . . PLAYED THE HARLOT: Continuing the marriage metaphor, God now begins to describe the spiritual harlotry of Israel from King Solomon (1 Kings 11:1) all the way to Ezekiel's time. God first provides a general summary of the nation's idolatry as she gave herself to the religious practices of the Canaanites. Every gracious gift from Him was devoted to idols.

20–22. SONS . . . DAUGHTERS: This refers to the sacrifices of children to pagan gods (see Ezekiel 20:25–26, 31; 2 Kings 16:3; 21:6; 23:10; 24:4). God had expressly forbidden this (see Deuteronomy 12:31; 18:10). Still, the children were first slain, then burned (see Jeremiah 7:31; 19:5; 32:35; Micah 6:7) until Josiah's abolition of it. It had been reinstated in Ezekiel's day.

23–30. A HIGH PLACE IN EVERY STREET: This section, partly woe and partly lament, spoke to Judah's obsession with idolatry and her being influenced by the people of Egypt (verse 26), by the Philistines (verse 27), by Assyria (verse 28), and by Babylon (verse 29).

27. PHILISTINES . . . WERE ASHAMED: The wickedness and gross evil of the Jews even scandalized pagan Philistines.

29. CHALDEA: The Jews had even prostituted themselves with the Babylonians (see 2 Kings 20:12–19).

31–34. PAYMENTS TO ALL YOUR LOVERS: It is wicked to solicit and then be paid for immoral deeds. But Israel engaged in far worse behavior—she solicited and even paid her idol consorts. This refers to the heavy tribute Israel had to pay to the godless nations.

35–40. I . . . WILL UNCOVER YOUR NAKEDNESS: Public exposure of profligate women and stoning them were well-known customs in ancient Israel, making prostitutes a shameful spectacle.

42. LAY TO REST MY FURY: By exacting the full penalty on Israel's sins in the destruction by Babylon, God's wrath was to be satisfied.

44–45. LIKE MOTHER, LIKE DAUGHTER: Judah had followed in the pagan footsteps of her beginnings (see Ezekiel 16:3).

46–59. YOUR ELDER SISTER IS SAMARIA: Judah is compared to Samaria and Sodom, whose judgments for sin were great. Judah was more corrupt (verse 47), multiplied Samaria's and Sodom's sin (verse 51), and committed more abominable sin (verse 52).

60. I WILL REMEMBER MY COVENANT: God is gracious and always finds a covenant basis on which He can exercise His grace. The Lord here says that He will remember the Abrahamic covenant made with Israel in her youth (see Genesis 12:1ff.). Restoration will be by grace, not by merit.

AN EVERLASTING COVENANT: This is the New Covenant, which is unconditional, saving, and everlasting (see Ezekiel 37:26; Isaiah 59:21; 61:8; Jeremiah 31:31–34; Hebrews 8:6–13). The basis of God's grace will not be the Mosaic covenant, which the Jews could never fulfill, even with the best intentions (see Exodus 24:1ff.). When God establishes His eternal covenant, Israel will know that God is the Lord because of His grace.

63. AN ATONEMENT: This looks to the cross of Christ (see Isaiah 53), by which God's just wrath on sin was satisfied so that He could grant grace to all who believe (see 2 Corinthians 5:21).

> THE EAGLES AND THE VINE: This next chapter in Ezekiel is dated to about 588 BC (two years before the destruction of Jerusalem). The history of the period is recounted in 2 Kings 24; 2 Chronicles 36; and Jeremiah 36; 37; 52.

17:3. A GREAT EAGLE: The king of Babylon, in view here, took royal captives and others (see verses 4, 12–13).

THE CEDAR: The kingdom of Judah.

4. TOPMOST YOUNG TWIG: This is Jehoiachin, the king, who was exiled in 597 BC (see 2 Kings 24:11–16). Babylon is the "land of trade" (16:29).

5–6. SEED: Those whom Babylon left behind in Judah (597 BC), who could prosper as a tributary to the conqueror.

6. A SPREADING VINE: This refers to Zedekiah (c. 597–586 BC), the youngest son of Josiah, whom Nebuchadnezzar appointed king in Judah. The benevolent attitude of Nebuchadnezzar helped Zedekiah to prosper, and if he had remained faithful to his pledge to Nebuchadnezzar, Judah would have continued as a tributary kingdom. Instead, he began courting help from Egypt (see 2 Chronicles 36:13), which Jeremiah protested (see Jeremiah 37:5–7).

7. ANOTHER GREAT EAGLE: Egypt is meant (see verse 15), specifically Pharaoh Apries (also known as Hophra; 588–568 BC). Zedekiah turned to him for help in revolting against Babylon.

9–10. WITHER: Zedekiah's treachery would not prosper. The king was captured in the plains of Jericho (see Jeremiah 52:8). Judah's dependence on Egypt would fail, and the nation would wither as the east wind (a picture of Babylon— see Ezekiel 13:11–13) blasted her.

11–21. PUT HIM UNDER OATH: The parable is now explained in detail. Babylon (verse 12) made Zedekiah a vassal subject to her, took captives, and left Judah weak (verses 13–14). Zedekiah broke the agreement (verse 15) in which he swore by the Lord to submit to Babylon (see 2 Chronicles 36:13). He instead sought Egypt's help; thus, he was taken to Babylon to live out his life (verses 16, 19; see also Jeremiah 39:4–7). Egypt was to be no help to him (verse 17) or a protector of his army (verse 21).

22–23. ONE OF THE HIGHEST BRANCHES: This messianic prophecy states that God will provide the Messiah from the royal line of David ("the high cedar") and establish Him in His kingdom (like a "prominent mountain"; see also Daniel 2:35, 44–45). He will be "a high branch" reigning at the height of success. "Branch" is a name for the Messiah (see Ezekiel 34:23–24; 37:24–25; Isaiah 4:2; Jeremiah 23:5; 33:15; Zechariah 3:8; 6:12). The Messiah will be "a tender one" (verse 22), growing into a "majestic cedar" (verse 23). Under His kingdom rule, all nations will be blessed and Israel restored.

24. MADE THE DRY TREE FLOURISH: The Messiah would grow out of the dry tree left after Judah's humbling judgment (that is, Judah's remnant), from which He came of a lowly family (see Isaiah 6:13), and yet would still prosper.

UNLEASHING THE TEXT

1) Idolatry is a key theme in Ezekiel 14–17. What is idolatry? Why is it harmful?

_____

_____

_____

_____

_____

_____

_____

2) What attitude does God express toward His people in Ezekiel 16:1–14? What do you learn from those verses about God's care and protection of His people?

_____

_____

_____

_____

_____

_____

_____

_____

3) What attitude does God express toward His people in Ezekiel 16:15–34? What do you learn from those verses about the Israelites' lack of faithfulness to God?

_____

_____

_____

_____

_____

_____

_____

4) Where do you see evidence for hope regarding Israel's future in these chapters?

_____

_____

_____

_____

_____

_____

_____

_____

_____

_____

_____

EXPLORING THE MEANING

God judges false teachers fervently. Chapter 14 describes an interesting moment in Ezekiel's ministry. A group of elders from Israel came to him, ostensibly to hear the word of the Lord. However, the Holy Spirit revealed to Ezekiel that these leaders had "set up their idols in their hearts" (verse 3). They were false teachers and false leaders in the community; therefore, God would not respond to their inquiries. Instead, He promised that all who embraced idolatry would experience judgment. The leaders of Israel and Judah had steered the people away from God and toward idols, which had led to devastating consequences. Later, during Jesus' public ministry, He likewise emphasized the dangers of false teachers and false prophets, saying, "Beware of false prophets, who come to you in sheep's clothing, but inwardly they are ravenous wolves" (Matthew 7:15). Our Savior also gave us a clear method for identifying false teachers: "You will know them by their fruits" (verse 16). In the church today, those who lead people toward righteousness and intimacy with God should be recognized as godly leaders. But those who lead people toward idolatry should be wholeheartedly rejected.

God loves His people intimately. In the church today, we often refer to God's "love" for His people. We describe how God loves His followers and how He loves the world. Yet if we are not careful, we can drift into thinking of God's love in general (or even generic) terms. Ezekiel 16, however, reveals that God's love is deeply intimate. Through His prophet, God described His love for Israel in terms of someone finding an abandoned baby and choosing to embrace it as a beloved child. The language here is deeply personal: "'When I passed by you again and looked upon you, indeed your time was the time of love; so I spread My wing over you and covered your nakedness. Yes, I swore an oath to you and entered into a covenant with you, and you became Mine,' says the Lord GOD" (verse 8). Because God is the same yesterday, today, and forever, we know that He draws near to us with this same intimate, personal love.

God provides for His people eternally. Ezekiel prophesied to a group of captives who had been removed from their land because of God's judgment, declaring that another round of judgment against Judah was imminent. Yet even in the midst of those sober messages, Ezekiel continually pointed forward to God's promises of hope for Israel as well as for all people. Near the end of chapter 16, God declared, "Nevertheless I will remember My covenant with you in the days of your youth, and I will establish an everlasting covenant with you" (verse 60). This everlasting covenant points forward to Jesus, the Messiah, and the covenant of salvation by grace through faith. Later, near the end of chapter 17, God promised to plant a branch "on the mountain height of Israel . . . and it will bring forth boughs, and bear fruit, and be a majestic cedar" (verse 23). Several Old Testament prophets likewise described the Messiah in terms of a branch that would grow and produce a mighty tree, which is another reference to Christ's kingdom during the Millennium. So, even in the midst of God carrying out His judgment against Israel, He made a point to remind His people that salvation and an eternal kingdom were on the horizon.

REFLECTING ON THE TEXT

5) What are some of the ways that false teachers operate today? What makes them so dangerous?

_____

_____

_____

_____

_____

_____

_____

_____

_____

6) Jesus said we can identify false teachers by their "fruit." What kind of fruit does a false teacher produce? What kind of fruit does a faithful teacher produce?

_____

_____

_____

_____

_____

_____

_____

7) God's words to His people in Ezekiel 16:1–14 reveal His deep and personal love for them. How has God shown that same love to you?

_____

_____

_____

_____

_____

_____

_____

8) God reminded His people that salvation and an eternal kingdom were on the horizon. How does this likewise reassure you as a child of God?

_____

_____

_____

_____

_____

_____

_____

PERSONAL RESPONSE

9) How do you discern whether a teaching you receive is true or false?

_____

_____

_____

_____

_____

_____

_____

_____

10) Who are three people in your life who need to hear God's message of salvation
    and eternal life? What would it take on your part to share that message with them?

_____

_____

_____

_____

_____

_____

_____

_____

_____

5

THE SWORD OF GOD
Ezekiel 18:1–21:32

DRAWING NEAR

Where have you felt the long-term consequences of sins in your life? What has that taught you about your responsibility for your own sins?

_____

_____

_____

_____

_____

_____

_____

_____

_____

_____

_____

_____

THE CONTEXT

In the law of Moses, God established that sin in one generation would produce consequences in subsequent generations. For instance, when God gave the Ten Commandments to Moses, He said: "I, the LORD your God, am a jealous God, visiting the iniquity of the fathers upon the children to the third and fourth generations of those who hate Me" (Exodus 20:5). Later, when Moses reviewed the Ten Commandments with the Israelites, he reminded them that God had indeed said, "For I, the LORD your God, am a jealous God, visiting the iniquity of the fathers upon the children to the third and fourth generations of those who hate Me" (Deuteronomy 5:9).

When we move forward in time to Ezekiel's day, we find that God's people were apparently using this principle to absolve themselves of blame for their current situation. They believed that their captivity, and the struggles that Judah had encountered as a whole, were the result of the sins of previous generations and thus there was nothing significant they could do to alter the situation. In Ezekiel 18 and 19, God specifically and directly rejects this way of thinking. The current generation of Israelites had themselves chosen rebellion and idolatry, which was the reason for their tribulations and exile from the promised land.

The early verses of Ezekiel 20 indicate that eleven months had passed between the end of one prophetic message (see 14:1–3) and the beginning of the next. During that time, we know from history that Egypt began to flex its power as a nation, resisting the advance of Babylon. King Zedekiah of Judah used Babylon's defeats during that time as an opportunity to launch his own rebellion (see 2 Kings 24:20). This rebellion ultimately failed, of course, resulting in the siege of Jerusalem and its eventual destruction at the hands of Nebuchadnezzar. However, it is likely that the "elders of Israel" who once again inquired of the prophet at the beginning of chapter 20 wanted to know if God was going to use Egypt as a tool to throw off the yolk of Babylon and return them, the captives, to their homeland of Judah.

KEYS TO THE TEXT
Read Ezekiel 18:1–21:32, noting the key words and phrases indicated below.

> A FALSE PROVERB REFUTED: *One of the foundational principles of Scripture (also taught in Deuteronomy 24:16 and 2 Kings 14:6) is presented in this chapter: God's judgment is rendered according to individual faith and conduct. God had foretold national punishment, but the basis for it was individual sin.*

18:2. EATEN SOUR GRAPES: The people of Judah would not acknowledge their guilt was worthy of judgment. Although they were themselves wicked and idolatrous, they blamed their forefathers for their current state (see 2 Kings 21:15). Their rationalizing was expressed in a proverb of the day (see Jeremiah 31:29) that meant, in effect, "They sinned (ate sour grapes); we inherited the bitterness (teeth set on edge)."

3. NO LONGER USE THIS PROVERB: God rejected the people's blame shifting and evasion of responsibility.

4. THE SOUL WHO SINS SHALL DIE: God played no favorites but was fair in holding each person accountable for his own sin. The "death" mentioned here is physical death, which, for many people, results in eternal death.

5–18. IF A MAN . . . BEGETS A SON: Two scenarios are proposed to clarify the matter of personal guilt: (1) a just father of an unjust son (verses 5–13); and (2) an unjust father of a just son (verses 14–18).

5. JUST: The definition of "just" or "righteous" is given specifically in verses 6–9. Such behavior could only characterize a genuine believer who was "faithful" from the heart.

8. EXACTED USURY: This refers to interest on loans. The prohibition of lending money at interest to a fellow Israelite is qualified by Exodus 22:25 and Leviticus 25:35–36, which indicates that it restricts its application to the poor and prevents further impoverishment, but it was allowed for foreigners who were engaged in trade and commerce to enlarge their wealth. According to Deuteronomy 15:1–2, it is also clear that money could be legitimately lent in the normal course of business, subject to forgiveness of all unpaid debt in the sabbatical year.

9. HE SHALL SURELY LIVE: The righteous do die physically for many reasons that do not contradict this principle—including old age, martyrdom, or death in battle. While there are exceptions to "surely live" as to temporal life (see Ezekiel 21:3–4), and sometimes the ungodly survive, unlike 18:13 (see 14:22–23), there can be absolutely no exceptions in God's ultimate spiritual reckoning. In every case, the just die to live eternally and the unjust, who never possessed spiritual life, shall perish physically and eternally (see John 5:28–29; Revelation 20:11–15). The just will live no matter what the character of their parents or children.

10–13. SON . . . A ROBBER: Could such a sinful son claim the merits of his father's righteousness and live? No! Each person is responsible for his own sin.

14–18. HE SHALL DIE FOR HIS INIQUITY: This features an unjust father and a just son to make the same point. The righteous son shall "surely live" (verse 17).

19–20. THE SOUL WHO SINS SHALL DIE: The prophet here restates the principle of personal accountability.

21–22. IF A WICKED MAN TURNS: The next case involves an unjust person turning to righteousness. He received a clean slate in forgiveness (verse 22) and spiritual life forever.

23. DO I HAVE . . . PLEASURE: God takes no willful pleasure in the death of the unrighteous (see John 5:40; 1 Timothy 2:4; 2 Peter 3:9).

24. A RIGHTEOUS MAN TURNS: The next scenario is a righteous man turning to a life of sin. His former apparent righteousness was not genuine (see 1 John 2:19), and God did not remember it as a valid expression of faith.

25–29. YET YOU SAY: God applied the principle in summary to Israel's sin problem (see verses 2–4). They—not He—must acknowledge their lack of equity (verses 25, 29).

30. THEREFORE I WILL JUDGE: The conclusion is that a just God must judge each person for his own life. But He invites repentance so that hope may replace ruin (see Ezekiel 33:10–11).

31. GET . . . A NEW HEART: The key to life eternal and triumph over death is conversion. This involves repentance from sin (verses 30–31a) and receiving the new heart that God gives with a new spirit, wrought by the Holy Spirit (see 36:24–27; Jeremiah 31:34; John 3:5–8).

32. I HAVE NO PLEASURE: The death of God's saints is precious to Him (see Psalm 116:15). By contrast, He has no pleasure when a person dies without repentance. While God is sovereign in salvation, man is responsible for his own sin.

THEREFORE TURN AND LIVE: This was a call for the people to repent and avoid physical and eternal death (see Psalms 23:6; 73:24; Isaiah 26:19–21; Daniel 12:2–3, 13). Ezekiel was a preacher of repentance and of God's offer of mercy to the penitent.

A LAMENT: The "lamentation" in this section is an elegy in typical lamentation meter (verse 14b), dealing with the captivity of Jehoahaz (609 BC) and Jehoiachin (597 BC), plus the collapse of the Davidic dynasty under Zedekiah (586 BC).

19:1. THE PRINCES OF ISRAEL: This refers to the kings of Judah who were just mentioned.

1–9. WHAT IS YOUR MOTHER: Judah is the "lioness," just as in verse 10 she is the "vine." Her cubs symbolize kings who were descendants of David exposed to the corrupting influences of heathen kings ("young lions").

3–4. ONE OF HER CUBS: This refers to Jehoahaz (Shallum), who ruled in 609 BC and was deposed by Egypt's Pharaoh Necho after reigning only three months (verse 4; see 2 Kings 23:32–34; 2 Chronicles 36:2).

5–9. ANOTHER OF HER CUBS: This refers to Jehoiachin, who in 597 BC was carried to Babylon in a cage, as in verse 9 (see 2 Kings 24:6–15). Although Jehoiachin reigned only three months, he was oppressive and unjust. God used the pagan nations of Egypt and Babylon to judge these wicked kings. The Babylonians kept Jehoiachin imprisoned for thirty-seven years, releasing him at the age of fifty-five (see 2 Kings 25:27–30; Jeremiah 52:31–32).

10–14. YOUR MOTHER . . . LIKE A VINE: Judah prospered as a luxuriant vine (verse 10), with strong power and eminence (verse 11). God plucked up the vine in judgment, desolating her (verse 12; see also Ezekiel 13:11–13), exiling her (verse 13), and leaving no strong king (verse 14).

14. A ROD: The blame for the catastrophe that came to Judah is laid on one ruler, King Zedekiah, who was responsible for the burning of Jerusalem because of his treachery (see Jeremiah 38:20–23). The house of David ended in shame and, for nearly 2,600 years after, Israel had no king of David's line. When the Messiah came, they rejected Him and preferred Caesar. The Messiah still became their Savior and will return as their King.

THE REBELLIONS OF ISRAEL: When certain "elders of Israel" come to Ezekiel to inquire of the Lord, he responds with a message from God that gives a historical survey of Israel, featuring its pattern of sin.

20:1. THE SEVENTH YEAR: Circa 591 BC.

3–44. ELDERS . . . CAME TO INQUIRE: See the similarity in Ezekiel 14:1–3. God's response to the elders describes how Israel rebelled in Egypt (verses 5–9), then in the wilderness trek (verses 10–26), and then when they entered into the land of promise (verses 27–32). Through all this, God kept delivering them to save His reputation (verses 9, 14, 22), yet their sinful obstinacy finally led to His judging them (verses 45–49). Verses 33–44 speak of God regathering Israel to their land in the future time of Christ's Second Advent.

5. RAISED MY HAND . . . OATH: See verses 5–6, 15, 23, 28, 42. God promised Israel deliverance from Egypt (see Exodus 6:2–8).

25–32. I . . . gave them up: God allowed the Jews to live in sin. They had said in their minds, "We will be like the Gentiles, like the families in other countries, serving wood and stone" (verse 32; see also Psalm 81:11–12; Romans 1:24–28). Like all human beings, the story of the Jews is one long history of rebellion.

34. I WILL BRING YOU OUT . . . GATHER YOU: Paul alludes to this in 2 Corinthians 6:17. God will someday rule over Israel in the glorious kingdom of the Messiah, after the people have repented and been saved (see Zechariah 12–14).

35–36. WILDERNESS OF THE PEOPLES: Other lands where the scattered people of Israel live are pictured as a wilderness in which the Jews will suffer (verse 35). This is analogous to God's bringing His people from Egypt through the wilderness long ago, before thrusting them into the promised land (verse 36).

37. PASS UNDER THE ROD: God uses a shepherd figure here, which is apt because He is their great Shepherd (see Ezekiel 34:11–13; Jeremiah 23:5–8). As a shepherd, God brings His sheep home to their fold (see Jeremiah 33:13), has them file in, and separates sheep from goats (see Matthew 25), passing under His shepherd's rod to be noted and checked for injury. He will bring them into the bond of the New Covenant by giving them His Spirit with life (see Ezekiel 36:24–27; 37:14; 39:29). This is Israel's final salvation (see Romans 11:26–33).

38. I WILL PURGE THE REBELS: God will see that no rebel—no one without the renewing by His Spirit in salvation—will come back to Palestine to have a part in the messianic kingdom. All whom He permits to return will serve Him (see verse 40), in contrast to those who serve idols (see verse 39). The purging takes place at the "time of Jacob's trouble" (Jeremiah 30:7), during the Great Tribulation (see Matthew 24:21).

39. GO, SERVE . . . HIS IDOLS: If the people persist in their stubborn idolatry, God will allow them to follow it to their doom. He would rather have them as out-and-out idolaters rather than hypocritical patronizers of His worship, like they had been (see Amos 5:21–26).

40–42. ALL . . . IN THE LAND: The promised regathering in the Messiah's earthly kingdom is to the very same land—literal Palestine—from which they were scattered (verse 41); expressly, the land given to their fathers (see Ezekiel 36:28; Genesis 12:7). They will all be there, repentant (verse 43), saved (see Romans 11:26–27), and serving the Lord wholeheartedly, a united nation engaged in purified worship (see Ezekiel 27:22–23; Isaiah 11:13).

44. YOU SHALL KNOW: God purposed all this great restoration so that repentant, renewed Israel knew that He was the Lord—a key theme, as in verse 38. Also, those of other nations would know by this who He was and render Him due reverence (see verse 41; 36:23, 36).

46–48. PREACH AGAINST THE SOUTH: The "south" is Palestine, particularly Judah, which was usually invaded from the north. Although Babylonia was to the east (see 19:12), its army would swing west toward the Mediterranean Sea and then come south out of the north to invade Judah. The invader (Nebuchadnezzar in 586 BC) would overwhelm the land as a sweeping fire (see 15:1–8; 19:12; Zechariah 11:1–3), devouring trees indiscriminately, green or dry (see Ezekiel 21:3–4). Palestine had much more forest in biblical times.

49. DOES HE NOT SPEAK IN PARABLES: This demonstrates the elders' (see verse 1) refusal to comprehend Ezekiel's clear message. To the unwilling heart, there was no understanding.

JUDGMENT LIKE A SWORD: God depicts His judgment against the people of Israel in terms of a man unsheathing his polished sword for deadly thrusts. God is the swordsman, and Babylon is His sword.

21:1. I WILL DRAW MY SWORD: The historical background for this prophecy is Nebuchadnezzar's 588 BC campaign to quell revolts in Judah, as well as Tyre and Ammon.

3–4. RIGHTEOUS AND WICKED: In Babylon's indiscrimination as an invader, people in the army's path will die, whether they are righteous or wicked. This occurs from north to south, through the whole span of Israel's land, tying in with the judgment that was previously pictured by fire (see 20:45–49). "Every green tree and every dry tree" (20:47) probably depicts these people, whether righteous or wicked (see Luke 23:31).

8–17. AGAIN THE WORD OF THE LORD CAME TO ME: God now tells Ezekiel that the sword (Babylon) is "sharpened."

10. IT DESPISES THE SCEPTER OF MY SON: See verse 13. Possibly, this affirms that God's sword, so overwhelming in verse 10a, was to despise the Judean royal scepter (see Genesis 49:9–10), which was powerless to stop it and would soon pass away (see Ezekiel 21:25–27). God's judgment was too strong for this object made of (or partly of) wood, as it holds in contempt all such items of wood. "My son" may refer to Judah (see Exodus 4:22–23) or to the king as God's "son," such as was Solomon (see 1 Chronicles 28:6).

11. SLAYER: God is always judge and executioner, no matter what He uses.

12. STRIKE YOUR THIGH: This can also be translated, "beat your breast." With either wording, it refers to an emphatic gesture of grief that the prophet acts out.

This accompanies further symbols of grief in his "cry," "wail" (verse 12), clapping of hands (see verse 14), and "beating of fists" (verse 17).

18–20. TWO WAYS . . . TO GO: This imagery portrays the Babylonians' army on the march coming to a crossroads. The sword is the king of Babylon, Nebuchadnezzar, who is faced with a decision. One sign points to Jerusalem and Judah, while the other points to Rabbah, the capital of Ammon. In 593 BC, Ammon had conspired with Judah against Babylon. The king had to decide which place to attack, so he sought his gods through divination (see verse 21).

21. THE KING . . . STANDS . . . TO USE DIVINATION: This means to "seek an omen," to gain guidance from superstitious devices (see Isaiah 47:8–15). Three methods of divination are available to Babylon's leader: (1) he can shake arrows, let them fall, and then read a conclusion from the pattern; (2) he can look at teraphim (idols); or (3) he can examine an animal liver to gain help from his gods. Actually, the true God is in control of this superstition to achieve His will—the attack on Jerusalem and Judah. Later, Nebuchadnezzar would attack Rabbah in Ammon, east of the Jordan (see Ezekiel 21:28–32).

22. BATTERING RAMS . . . SIEGE MOUND . . . WALL: All the paraphernalia of war are prepared.

23. LIKE A FALSE DIVINATION: The people of Jerusalem thought this superstitious decision was not a true divination and would fail. They were wrong (see verses 24–25).

25. WICKED PRINCE: This is Zedekiah (597–586 BC).

26. REMOVE . . . TURBAN . . . CROWN: God, in the coming judgment of Judah in 588–586 BC, removed the "turban" representing the priestly leadership and the "crown" picturing the succession of kings. Neither office was fully restored after the captivity. This marked the commencement of "the times of the Gentiles" (Luke 21:24).

27. UNTIL HE COMES: The threefold mention of "overthrown" expresses the severest degree of unsettled and chaotic conditions. Israel was to experience severe instability, and even the kingly privilege would be revoked until the Messiah came, "to whom it rightly belongs," or "whose right it is"(see Genesis 49:10). God would give the kingship to Him (see Jeremiah 23:5–8), the greater "David" (Ezekiel 37:24). His "right" is that perfect combination of priestly and royal offices (see Hebrews 5–7).

28–32. CONCERNING THE AMMONITES: The Babylonian armies were to also conquer this people in 582/581 BC (see Ezekiel 25:1–7). Their "reproach" was the gleeful disdain they heaped on Jerusalem when the city fell, the temple was profaned, and the Judeans were taken captive (see 25:3).

30. RETURN IT TO ITS SHEATH: The Ammonites were not to resist Babylon, which would be useless, for they would be slaughtered in their own land.

32. YOU SHALL NOT BE REMEMBERED: Israel had a future (see verse 27), but God would not give Ammon mercy at the time and would allow the devastation to occur. After this, the Ammonites were further devastated by Judas Maccabeus's army, according to an ancient source (1 Maccabees 5:6–7). Later, according to Jeremiah 49:6, God permitted exiles to return to their land. Finally, they disappeared from the family of nations altogether.

UNLEASHING THE TEXT

1) What principle did the Lord establish while speaking to the Jewish captives in Ezekiel 18:3–9?

_____

_____

_____

_____

_____

2) What step did God want those same captives to take in Ezekiel 18:19–32?

_____

_____

_____

_____

3) God offered a history lesson to the Israelites in Ezekiel 20:1–32. How would you summarize that lesson in a few sentences?

_____

_____

_____

_____

_____

4)   Imagine you were one of the captives of Judah when you heard God's declaration in Ezekiel 21:1–17. How would you respond to those words?

_____

_____

_____

_____

_____

Exploring the Meaning

God's methods of judgment are just. The captives living in Babylon had apparently begun to feel that God was treating them unjustly. They quoted a proverb implying that God was punishing them because of the transgressions of earlier generations: "The fathers have eaten sour grapes, and the children's teeth are set on edge" (Ezekiel 18:2). God rejected these claims and, in so doing, established a critical principle: people are judged on their individual faith and conduct toward Him, not on the nation in which they live or the community into which they were born. "'If [a man] has walked in My statutes and kept My judgments faithfully—he is just; he shall surely live!' says the Lord God" (verse 9). Conversely, if someone chooses to reject God and embrace a life of oppression, violence, greed, and other forms of idolatry, "he shall surely die; his blood shall be upon him" (verse 13).

God's motives for judgment are just. In Ezekiel 14:1–3, several elders from among the captives approached the prophet and requested that he inquire of the Lord on their behalf. God refused even to hear their request, labeling them as false leaders of the people. A little less than a year later, the pattern repeats itself in Ezekiel 20. We do not know the identity of "the elders of Israel" (verse 1) who sat before Ezekiel this time, but we know they were again seeking a word from God. Specifically, they wanted to be told that God would soon relent from His judgment and return them to the promised land. Instead, God provided a history lesson of Israel's rebellion. He reminded them of the oaths and covenants made between Himself and Israel, which Israel had abandoned. He reminded them of how He had rescued them from Egypt and given His law, which Israel had rejected. He reminded them of their blasphemy and idolatry. Importantly, God was not saying the current generation of Israelites were being punished because of the transgressions of previous generations. Instead, He was showing how the current generation had continued those same transgressions, resulting in judgment.

God's means of judgment are just. Ezekiel's primary audience for the prophecies covered in this lesson were the tens of thousands of Jews who had been taken captive to Babylon. This audience was thus quite familiar with the Babylonians as a people—and especially with the Babylonian armies under King Nebuchadnezzar. Even so, God gave Ezekiel a terrifying prophesy identifying those armies as God's "sword," which He would use to complete His judgment against Judah and Jerusalem. "Thus says the LORD: 'Behold, I am against you, and I will draw My sword out of its sheath and cut off both righteous and wicked from you'" (Ezekiel 21:3). The captives hoped God would remove the threat of Babylon. Instead, God said that He was directing the forces of Babylon at Jerusalem (see verses 18–27). The principle here is that God is sovereign over all things, including nations and kings. The Babylonians were the supreme might of the day, yet they existed merely as a sword in God's hands to be used for His purposes.

REFLECTING ON THE TEXT

5) What are some of the ways that people accuse God of being unfair today? What are the problems with such accusations?

_____

_____

_____

_____

_____

_____

6) In Ezekiel 18, God established the principle that He judges individuals based on their condition before God. How does that principle relate to the gospel?

_____

_____

_____

_____

_____

7) The Bible does state that the sins of one generation are often continued (or even expounded) by succeeding generations. Where do you see that reality today?

_____

_____

_____

_____

_____

_____

8) How does God's use of the Babylonians to judge Israel help to explain the outworking of His sovereignty?

_____

_____

_____

_____

_____

PERSONAL RESPONSE

9) Where are you currently in danger of continuing the cycles of sinful behavior from your parents or grandparents?

_____

_____

_____

_____

_____

10) What are some steps you can take to eliminate those sins from your life?

_____

_____

_____

_____

_____

_____

6

TWO UNFAITHFUL SISTERS

Ezekiel 22:1–25:17

DRAWING NEAR

Why is unfaithfulness so devastating? Why is it so much worse when committed against a faithful party?

_____

_____

_____

_____

_____

_____

_____

_____

_____

_____

_____

_____

_____

_____

_____

_____

_____

THE CONTEXT

As we begin this lesson, it will be helpful to take a brief step back to remember the broader context of the Jewish people in the promised land. What was initially established as the nation of Israel had thrived under the kingship of David and

Solomon. However, that nation was divided after Solomon's death. Two tribes, Benjamin and Judah, established the southern kingdom of Judah, which included the city of Jerusalem. The remaining ten tribes rebelled against David's house and established the northern kingdom of Israel.

The Bible reveals that the northern kingdom of Israel was continuously rebellious against God and turned to idolatry in many different forms. As a result, it was conquered by the Assyrians in 721 BC. The Israelites were largely removed from the land, and people of other nations were brought in—a devastating punishment for those who had been in covenant with God. The southern kingdom of Judah struggled back and forth between periods of righteousness and idolatry. However, even during times of rebellion, the residents of Judah believed they would permanently reside under God's protection because of Jerusalem, the holy city, and the temple in which God had allowed His name to dwell.

After the conquest of the kingdom of Israel, the people of Judah should have recognized the precariousness of their position in the land. However, the nation continued on a downward spiral spiritually until Babylon forced the payment of homage in 605 BC and then attacked Jerusalem in 597 BC. This attack is when the captives, including Ezekiel, were removed from Judah and taken to Babylon. Even so, both the captives and the residents of Judah still refused to repent. Jerusalem was ultimately destroyed about ten years later in 586 BC.

KEYS TO THE TEXT

Read Ezekiel 22:1–25:17, noting the key words and phrases indicated below.

> THE SINS OF JERUSALEM: *God indicts Jerusalem's "blood guiltiness." The only restraint on their evil was the limits of their ability to sin. They did all the evil they could—and the shedding of blood seemed to be the most popular.*

22:2. THE BLOODY CITY: This phrase refers to Jerusalem because of her judicial murders (see verses 6, 9, 23–27), her sacrifice of children, and her rebellion against Babylon (see 24:6).

4–13. BECOME GUILTY: At least seventeen kinds of sin appear in God's indictment against Jerusalem, with more given in verses 25–29.

5. THOSE NEAR AND FAR . . . WILL MOCK YOU: See Romans 2:24. God links His honor to the behavior of His people.

9. EAT ON THE MOUNTAINS: This refers to idol worship, which the passage clarifies (see verse 4); that is, eating meals at idol shrines accompanied by sexual sins, such as those described in verses 10–11.

14–16. I WILL SCATTER YOU: Ezekiel saw not only the punishment of the Jews in the immediate future but also the worldwide dispersion of the Jews that is still going on today, which continues for the purging of Israel's sins.

16. YOU SHALL KNOW: After the defiling dispersion, when the sin has been purged, Israel will come to know the Lord. Many Jews do know Him now, but the nation will be saved in the future (see Zechariah 12–14; Romans 11:25–27).

17–22. BRONZE, TIN, IRON, AND LEAD: This pictures God's judgment of Jerusalem as a smelting furnace (see Isaiah 1:22; Jeremiah 6:28–30; Zechariah 13:9; Malachi 3:2–3), which burns away dross and impurities, resulting in purified metal. God's wrath was the fire (verse 21; an apt term for Babylon's fiery destruction of the city), His people were to be refined (verse 20), and the sinful ones were to be removed as dross (see 21:13–22). Even in the ultimate day, God will follow this principle in purging His creation of sin (see 2 Peter 3:9–14).

25–29. CONSPIRACY: The whole nation was wicked. First, all leaders are indicted for their vicious sin—prophets, priests, and princes—and then the people in general are accused.

30. SO I SOUGHT FOR A MAN: Prophets such as Ezekiel and Jeremiah were faithful, but apart from them, God sought a man capable of advocacy for Israel when its sin had gone so far. However, no one could lead the people to repentance and draw the nation back from the brink of the judgment that came in 586 BC (see Jeremiah 7:26, 36; 19:15). Only God's Messiah—God Himself—could have the character and the credentials sufficient to do what no mortal man could do: intercede for Israel (see Isaiah 59:16–19; 63:5; Revelation 5). Christ was rejected by the Jewish people during His earthly ministry, so the effects of this judgment continue today, until they turn to Him in faith (see Zechariah 12:10; 13:1).

TWO HARLOT SISTERS: *This chapter describes the spiritual infidelity of the people Israel and Judah, pictured here as two sisters, to convey the gravity of the sin in Judah.*

23:2–4. TWO WOMEN . . . ONE MOTHER: "One mother" refers to the united kingdom, while "two women" refers to the divided kingdom. Oholah, meaning "her own tabernacle," as she had her separate dwelling-place apart from the temple, represents Samaria. In the northern kingdom, Jeroboam had set up worship, which God rejected. Oholibah, "My tabernacle is in her," represents Jerusalem, where God did establish worship.

5–10. OHOLAH PLAYED THE HARLOT: The northern kingdom of Israel was a harlot, in a spiritual sense, by seeking a military and political union for fulfillment and security purposes with idolatrous, young, wealthy, attractive Assyria, who ultimately turned on Israel (verse 10), conquered her, and deported her people in 722 BC (see 2 Kings 17).

11–21. MORE CORRUPT: See Ezekiel 16:47. The focus is Judah's (the southern kingdom's) craving for Babylonian idolatry that alienated her from God. Judah learned nothing from Israel's punishment (see verse 13).

12. ASSYRIANS: Ahaz placed Judah under the protection of Assyria (see 2 Kings 16:7–10), a political move denounced by Isaiah (see Isaiah 7:13–17).

14–16. MEN PORTRAYED ON THE WALL: Judah was drawn to portraits of Babylonian men, done in brilliant colors, lusting for the Chaldean lifestyle. Their social and political alliance led to spiritual defection.

17. INTO THE BED OF LOVE: This description graphically portrays spiritual unfaithfulness (see Ezekiel 23:30).

19. PLAYED THE HARLOT IN THE LAND OF EGYPT: Judah renewed her old sins from the days of Egypt, returning to her first degradation.

22–35. STIR UP YOUR LOVERS: God's anger at Judah's sin prompted Him to bring the Babylonians and others to deal severely with her. This passage sets forth how Judah's companion nations were the instruments of her judgment.

23. PEKOD, SHOA, KOA: Three different Aramean tribes.

25. REMOVE YOUR NOSE . . . YOUR EARS: Atrocities by the Babylonians would include facial dismemberment, the ancient punishment for an adulteress practiced in Egypt, Chaldea, and elsewhere.

32–34. DRINK OF YOUR SISTER'S CUP: Judah was to experience the "cup" of God's judgment, as Samaria had in 722 BC (see 23:46–49). Often, the idea of drinking a cup is symbolic of receiving God's wrath (see Psalm 75:8; Isaiah 51:17–22; Jeremiah 25:15–29; Matthew 20:22).

36–42. DECLARE TO THEM THEIR ABOMINATIONS: The prophet here details a shameful summary of God's case against the nation—a double arraignment calling for judgment.

45. RIGHTEOUS MEN: This likely refers to the remnant of godly people in the nation who would affirm the justice of God's judgment.

SYMBOL OF THE COOKING POT: *The time of this prophecy was January 15, 588 BC (dating from 597 BC, as in Ezekiel 1:2). The Babylonians had begun the eighteen-month siege of Jerusalem (see Jeremiah 39:1–2; 52:4–12).*

24:3–5. UTTER A PARABLE: The choice cuts of lamb picture God's flock being boiled in a pot, symbolizing Jerusalem in the heat of the siege (see Ezekiel 11:3). Animal bones were frequently used for fuel.

6. WOE TO THE BLOODY CITY: Jerusalem's populace was guilty of bloody corruption, which was pictured by the boiled scum or rust in the pot (see 22:2).

7. HER BLOOD: The city's blood (a general symbol of sin) was blatantly open, not hidden, as depicted by exposure on top of a rock. When blood was not covered with dust, the law was violated (see Leviticus 17:13). God's vengeance would come by Babylon's army.

9–10. MAKE THE PYRE GREAT . . . LET THE CUTS BE BURNED UP: Intensely provoked by sin, God wanted Ezekiel to picture the fire as furious judgment that kills the people.

11–12. SET THE POT EMPTY: After all the pieces (people) were burned up, the pot was then heated empty. This portrayed the Lord's thorough follow-through, using the besieger to destroy the city and the temple, with all its residue. (See the treatment of a leprous house in Leviticus 14:34–45.)

16–27. I TAKE AWAY FROM YOU THE DESIRE OF YOUR EYES: The Lord here proclaimed to Ezekiel that his wife died as a sign to Israel. All personal sorrow was eclipsed in the universal calamity. Just as Ezekiel was not to mourn the death of his wife (verse 17), so Israel was not to mourn the death of her families (verses 19–24). Although the text emphasizes how precious Ezekiel's wife was to him—she was the "desire of his eyes" (verses 16, 21) and his "boast" and "delight" (verse 21)—the prophet was obedient and submitted to God's will. He became a heartbreaking sign to his people.

25. IN THE DAY: This refers to the destruction of the temple.

26–27. ON THAT DAY: A person who escaped the destruction of Jerusalem (586 BC) would come to Ezekiel in Babylon and report the story. From that day forward, he was to be silent until the captives arrived; then he could speak of Judah (see 3:26–27). This amounted to about a two-year period (see 33:21; Jeremiah 52:5–7), when there was no need to preach judgment because it had come. He did speak of other nations (beginning in Ezekiel 25).

PROCLAMATIONS AGAINST AMMON AND MOAB: God now proclaims His judgment on the Ammonites, who were located east of the Jordan River, and the Moabites, who lived south of the Arnon River along the lower region of the Dead Sea.

25:1. THE WORD OF THE LORD CAME: In Ezekiel 25:1–32:32, God proclaims judgments on seven nations other than Israel, similar to the series found in Jeremiah 46–51. Four of these nations are singled out in Ezekiel 25 for vindictive jealousy and hate toward Israel. It is fitting, after devoting Ezekiel 1–24 to calamity on His chosen nation, that God should reveal His impartiality toward all sinners and provide Ezekiel with judgments to proclaim on Gentiles. Israel's sinful failure had profaned God's honor in the eyes of these peoples (see 36:21–23), but they had falsely assumed that when Israel was exiled, their God was defeated.

2–3. AGAINST THE AMMONITES: These people lived on the edge of the desert, north of Moab. They had joined Babylon against Judah about 600 BC (see 2 Kings 24:2ff.). In 594 BC, together with other nations, they tried to influence Judah to ally with them against Babylon (see Jeremiah 27:2ff.). In Ezekiel 21:18–20, God indicates that the Babylonians came after them. There is no record of an attack, so they must have surrendered (see Ezekiel 21:28; Zephaniah 2:8–11). They were of incestuous origin (see Genesis 19:37–38) and often hostile toward Judah (see Judges 10; 1 Samuel 11; 2 Samuel 10, 12; Jeremiah 49:1–6; Lamentations 2:15; Amos 1:13–15). God judged the Ammonites because of their enmity against Israel (see Ezekiel 25:3, 6). They expressed malicious pleasure at the dishonoring of the temple, desolation of the land, and dispersion of the inhabitants.

4. I WILL DELIVER YOU . . . TO THE MEN OF THE EAST: This perhaps refers to the coming of Babylon from the east, which would devastate Ammon in either 588–586 BC or 582/581 BC. Or it could refer to the Ammonites' land being occupied by the various nomadic tribes living beyond the Jordan River.

5. RABBAH: This important Ammonite capitol (see Amos 1:14), now called Amman, is about twenty-five miles northeast of the upper tip of the Dead Sea, east of the Jordan River.

7. CAUSE YOU TO PERISH: The Ammonites would be destroyed and eliminated from their land. Yet Jeremiah 49:6 assures a later return of a remnant of these scattered people.

8–11. MOAB: The origin of these people is given in Genesis 19:37–38. The Moabites' land was the area along the lower region of the Dead Sea (see Isaiah

15; 16; Jeremiah 48; Amos 2:1–3). The Babylonians destroyed cities there in 582/581 BC. The reason for their judgment (verse 8) also included their gloating over Israel's fall, as well as their scorn in saying that Israel was like all other people with no privileged position before God. Both the Ammonites and Moabites became absorbed into the Arabian peoples.

Seir: Another name for the adjacent Edomite area (see Genesis 32:3; 36:20–21, 30), dominated by Mount Seir and a mountainous, extremely rugged, rocky country. Her judgments are given in Ezekiel 25:12–14.

Proclamations Against Edom and Philistia: *The Edomites lived south of Moab from the Dead Sea to the Gulf of Aqab. The Philistines resided to the west of Israel along the coast of the Mediterranean Sea.*

12. Edom: See Ezekiel 35; Isaiah 21:11–12; Jeremiah 49:7–22; Amos 1:11–12; Obadiah 1; Malachi 1:3–5. The Edomite people had almost been annihilated by David during his reign (see 2 Samuel 8:14), but they had won back their independence during the rule of King Ahaz (c. 735–715 BC). Their revenge was constant hostility toward Israel (see Genesis 27:27–41; Isaiah 34:5–7). The reason for judgment was Edom's disdain when the Israelites were devastated in 588–86 BC. They acted like a cheering section for Babylon, calling out, "raze it, raze it" (Psalm 137:7; Lamentations 4:21–22).

13–14. against Edom . . . by the hand of My people Israel: The Arab tribe of the Nabateans invaded Edom in 325 BC, but it was the Jewish forces under Judas Maccabeus in 164 BC and John Hyrcanus in 126 BC that fully subjugated Edom. The Jews even compelled the Edomites to submit to their religion. All three of these nations (Ammon, Moab, and Edom) have disappeared as separate nations, being absorbed into the Arab peoples.

13. Teman; Dedan: This reference is to key Edomite towns. Teman (Teima) was possibly 200 miles east of the Dead Sea in the Arabian Desert, located in the northern expanse of Edom's territory. Dedan is thought to have been located 100 miles south of Teman, yet far east of the Red Sea.

15–17. the Philistines: See Isaiah 14:29–33; Jeremiah 47; Joel 3:4; Amos 1:6–8; Obadiah 19; Zephaniah 2:4–7; Zechariah 9:5. The reason for the Philistines' judgment was perpetual enmity and vengefulness against Israel, which perpetuated the "old hatred" from as far back as Judges 13–16. They constantly harassed and oppressed Israel until David broke their power during Saul's reign (see

1 Samuel 17). They repeatedly rose up and were subdued by Israel. Nebuchad-nezzar invaded their land (see Jeremiah 47).

16. CHERETHITES: This people group originated in Crete and became part of the Philistine nation, with some serving in David's bodyguard (see 2 Samuel 8:18; 15:18).

17. GREAT VENGEANCE: This was fulfilled at the time of Babylon's invasion of 588–586 BC or 582/581 BC (see Jeremiah 25:20; 47:1–7).

UNLEASHING THE TEXT

1) Based on God's words to His prophet in Ezekiel 22, what are some of the ways the people of Judah had rejected their covenant with God?

_____

_____

_____

_____

_____

_____

2) In Ezekiel 22:23–31, the prophet specifically addresses Israel's wicked leaders. What had those leaders done to turn the nation away from the Lord?

_____

_____

_____

_____

_____

3) What was the point of God's story about the "two women" in Ezekiel 23? What was He communicating to His people through that story?

_____

_____

_____

_____

_____

4) What images do you find most striking in Ezekiel 24:3–14? Why did God instruct Ezekiel not to mourn the death of his wife in 24:15–27?

_____

_____

_____

_____

_____

_____

_____

EXPLORING THE MEANING

Judah had a problem with injustice. The corruption of Judah—and especially that of its leaders—is a main theme of Ezekiel 22. Ezekiel accused them of shedding innocent blood, even referring to Jerusalem as "the bloody city" (verse 2). Ezekiel also accused them of oppressing strangers, widows, and orphans (see verse 7), of "lewdness" (verse 9), and "extortion" (verse 12). In short, the people of Judah had rejected God's character and instead pursued all manner of wickedness in order to increase their power and wealth. This went hand in hand with their neglect of God's law, which called them to reject all idolatry and immorality and pursue holiness of heart and of hands. Their reversal of these requirements demanded God's punishment.

Judah had a problem with unfaithfulness. A root cause of Judah's spiritual failure was idolatry—specifically, the people's continuing decision to worship false gods rather than the one true God. Ezekiel portrayed this spiritual unfaithfulness in an extended parable about two sisters: (1) Oholah, representing the northern kingdom of Israel; and (2) Oholiab, representing Judah. According to God, both sisters "committed harlotry" (Ezekiel 23:3). But even more shocking, God declared that Oholiab, who represented Judah, was "more corrupt in her lust than [Israel], and in her harlotry more corrupt than her sister's harlotry" (verse 11). In other words, Judah was more spiritually corrupt than Israel. Instead of repenting of their idolatry, the people had turned to Babylonian gods and Babylonian lifestyles. As a result, God would give them what they craved: "Behold, I will stir up your lovers against you, from whom you have alienated yourself, and I will bring them against you from every side. . . . And they shall come against you with chariots, wagons, and war-horses, with a horde of people" (verses 22, 24).

Judah had a problem with pride. The second half of Ezekiel 24 contains a surprising object lesson commanded by God and carried out by His prophet. This object lesson revolved around the death of Ezekiel's wife: "Son of man, behold, I take away from you the desire of your eyes with one stroke; yet you shall neither mourn nor weep, nor shall your tears run down" (verse 16). God was true to His word, and Ezekiel's wife died the very next day. Obviously, this was a difficult assignment for the prophet, who loved his wife, yet that assignment came with a purpose. In the same way Ezekiel refused to mourn for his wife, the captives in Judah would hear about the destruction of Jerusalem and the temple—and would be unable to mourn. The people's pride had led them to believe God would never allow harm against His holy city or against His temple. Therefore, they had become dangerously complacent, even to the point of harboring idolatry and injustice. Similarly, we must not become complacent in our status as God's children and thereby allow ourselves to harbor sin in our lives.

REFLECTING ON THE TEXT

5) The leaders of Judah not only tolerated the abandonment of God's law but also perpetrated it. They selfishly took any course of action that served their interests rather than the interests of God and others. How can believers today make sure that they do not do the same?

_____

_____

_____

_____

_____

6) What does this passage reveal about how the Lord expects believers in Christ to treat other people?

_____

_____

_____

_____

_____

7) The Bible is clear that idolatry is sin. However, we often don't detect the presence of idolatry in our own lives. How can you know when you are drifting toward the worship of false gods?

_____

_____

_____

_____

_____

_____

_____

8) What are some symptoms of pride among followers of Christ today? In other words, what does the "fruit" of pride look like in the life of a Christian?

_____

_____

_____

_____

_____

_____

PERSONAL RESPONSE

9) Often, we do not understand the gravity of our sin. When was the last time you were cut to the heart about your sin? How does genuine mourning over sin cause us to grasp God's grace?

_____

_____

_____

_____

_____

_____

_____

_____

10) Where are you in danger of allowing pride to influence or damage your spiritual life with Christ?

_____

_____

_____

_____

_____

_____

_____

_____

7

LAMENTATION FOR TYRE AND EGYPT

Ezekiel 26:1–32:32

DRAWING NEAR

What obligation do people of every nation have to God? Are all people accountable to God?

_____

_____

_____

_____

_____

_____

_____

_____

_____

_____

_____

_____

_____

_____

THE CONTEXT

The entirety of the first half of Ezekiel's prophetic message from the Lord is directed toward the people of Judah, including both the captives living in Babylon and the residents still living in Judah and Jerusalem. However, the message takes a turn in chapter 25 through chapter 32. This section of Ezekiel's prophecies deal with foreign nations. Specifically, God proclaimed judgment against seven nations because of their rejection of Him and their oppression of His people.

Ezekiel 25 contains proclamations of judgment against the people groups living in Ammon, Moab, Edom, and Philistia. Each of these nations would experience the Lord's vengeance. Ezekiel 26–28 contains prophecies against Tyre and Sidon, which were seafaring nations that operated a commercial hub in the Mediterranean Sea. Ezekiel 29–32 includes judgments against the nation of Egypt, which, of course, had a long history with Israel by Ezekiel's day. Judah had once even sought to ally itself with Egypt against Assyria, but Egypt was a faulty partner (see 2 Kings 18:17–25).

So, what was the reason for God to proclaim His judgments against these nations at this point in Ezekiel's ministry? The placement of these chapters is likely due to Ezekiel's shocking announcement in chapter 24: "Son of man, write down the name of the day, this very day—the king of Babylon started his siege against Jerusalem this very day" (verse 2). God told Ezekiel that Jerusalem was under siege—news that normally would not have reached the captives in Babylon for many months. Now that God's judgment against Judah was underway, He turned His attention to the surrounding nations who were also guilty of great sin.

Keys to the Text

Read Ezekiel 26:1–32:32, noting the key words and phrases indicated below.

Proclamations Against Tyre: The judgments against this Phoenician city cover three chapters (Ezekiel 26–28), indicating its importance to God.

26:1. THE ELEVENTH YEAR: In 586 BC, the eleventh year of Jehoiachin's captivity, on the tenth day of the fifth month, Jerusalem was captured.

3. TYRE: Tyre was an ancient city of the Phoenicians, located on the coast of the Mediterranean Sea and on a nearby island bastion. The name of the city appears for the first time in the Bible in Joshua 19:29. The city had great influence during the reigns of David and Solomon. Hiram, its king, was a friend to David (see 2 Samuel 5:11) and helped him and Solomon in building operations (see 1 Kings 5:1–12; 1 Chronicles 14:1; 2 Chronicles 2:3, 11). Later, the Tyrians sold

Jews into slavery (see Joel 3:4–8; Amos 1:9–10). In Ezekiel's day, Tyre was the commercial center of the Mediterranean (see Ezekiel 27:3).

4. DESTROY THE WALLS OF TYRE: God would cause "many nations" (verse 3) to invade Tyre in successive attacks pictured as wave following wave. Babylon (see verse 7) besieged Tyre from 585–573 BC; later came Alexander's Grecian army in 332 BC. Babylon devastated the coastal city, but many Tyrians escaped to an island fortress, which withstood attack. The later Grecian attackers would "scrape" all the remaining "dust" and rubble and dump it into the sea, building a causeway to the island nearly one-half mile out. They also brought ships and overcame the fortress defenders in a devastating assault on Tyre. The predictions in Ezekiel 26–28 have thus been fulfilled with amazing literal accuracy.

5, 14. FOR SPREADING NETS: Tyre became a fishing city, a place to spread fishing nets for centuries, until the Saracens finally destroyed what was left in the fourth century. Since that time, the once great center of Mediterranean commerce has been a nondescript village.

7–14. I WILL BRING AGAINST TYRE ... NEBUCHADNEZZAR ... KING OF KINGS: Ezekiel here provides a vivid description of the original devastation by Babylon's King Nebuchadnezzar, who was called "king of kings" (verse 7) because so many of the other rulers were subject to him. God had given Nebuchadnezzar universal rule (see Daniel 2:37). Verses 8 and 9 describe the siege, while verses 10–14 describe the devastation.

12. THEY WILL PLUNDER: "Nebuchadnezzar" is named in verse 7, and "he" and "his" refer to him in verses 8–11, but "they" in verse 12 appears to broaden the reference to others among the "many nations" (verse 3). At this point, "they" refers to not only the Babylonians but also to Alexander's army, which later heaped debris from the ruins into the sea to advance to the island stronghold (see Zechariah 9:3–4).

13. SOUND OF YOUR SONGS ... HARPS: According to Isaiah 23:16, Tyre was famous for musicians.

15–18. THE PRINCES OF THE SEA WILL COME DOWN: Such an important center of commerce such as Tyre could not be destroyed without affecting all the nearby nations. All the nations around the Mediterranean would consider Tyre's fall a calamity. According to customs of mourning, rulers would descend from their thrones and disrobe.

19–21. WITH THOSE WHO DESCEND INTO THE PIT: Tyre's destruction is compared to a dead person placed in the grave.

LAMENTATION FOR TYRE: Ezekiel 27 is a lamentation for Tyre, in which God describes the city as a trade ship destroyed on the high seas. The proper names indicate the participants in commerce with Tyre.

27:5–9. FIR TREES FROM SENIR: The area is the Amorite designation for Mount Hermon, located to the northeast of the northern tip of the Sea of Galilee. Lesser known places were Elishah (verse 7), believed to be in Cyprus; Arvad (verse 8), an island city off the Mediterranean coast north of Byblos; and Gebal (verse 9), a name also used for Byblos, north of modern-day Beirut. The "Ashurites" (verse 6) were the Assyrians, who had skilled woodworkers.

10. MEN OF WAR: These places provided mercenary soldiers for the Phoenician army to defend Tyre.

11. GAMMAD: A place often identified as northern Syria.

12. TARSHISH: This verse begins the description of the commercial glory of Tyre. Most likely, this place refers to Tarshishah in southern Spain, a Phoenician colony that was famous for silver (see Jeremiah 10:9).

13. JAVAN, TUBAL, AND MESHECH: Javan was Ionia, a large area in Greece. The other two locations, in Asia Minor, may be the Tibarenoi and Moschoi mentioned by the writer Herodotus, or slave-trading cities called Tabal and Mushku by the Assyrians.

14. HOUSE OF TOGARMAH: Beth-Togarmah is identified with Armenia in northeast Asia Minor, which is modern-day Turkey.

15. DEDAN: A better textual reading would be Rhodes.

17. MINNITH: An Ammonite town (see Judges 11:33).

18. HELBON: Today it is called Halbun (or Halboun), located thirteen miles north of Damascus.

19. DAN: A Jewish Danite area is not meant; rather, this possibly refers to the city of Aden on the Persian Gulf.

CASSIA: A perfume.

20. DEDAN: See note on Ezekiel 25:13.

21. KEDAR: This refers to nomadic Bedouin tribes.

22. SHEBA AND RAAMAH: These were cities in the southwest extremity of Arabia (see Genesis 10:7; 1 Chronicles 1:9).

23. HARAN, CANNEH, EDEN: All were Mesopotamian towns; Canneh may have been in northern Syria, the Calneh of Amos 6:2, or the Caino of Isaiah 10:9.

ASSYRIA . . . CHILMAD: These were also in Mesopotamia.

25. SHIPS OF TARSHISH: This refers to the large cargo-carrying sea ships that sailed across the Mediterranean Sea.

26–27. THE EAST WIND BROKE: This pictures Tyre's fall aptly as a shipwreck on the seas. The sea, the place of her glory, will be her grave. "The east wind" is a picture of Babylon in its power from the east (see Ezekiel 13:11–13).

28–35. THE CRY: This maintains the metaphor of Tyre as a ship and turns particularly to people lamenting her ruin, because their livelihood has been tied to the commerce she represents. Verses 30–32 describe common actions signifying mourning.

36. HISS AT YOU: There will be some people who scorn with malicious joy.

PROCLAMATION AGAINST THE KING OF TYRE: *Ezekiel now declares a prophecy from God specifically against the king (or prince) of Tyre.*

28:1–19. SAY TO THE PRINCE OF TYRE: This section concerning the king of Tyre is similar to Isaiah 14:3–23, where the prophet refers to the king of Babylon. In both passages, some of the language best fits Satan. Most likely, both texts primarily describe the human king who is being used by Satan, much like Peter was being used when Jesus said to him, "Get behind Me, Satan!" (Matthew 16:23). The judgment given can certainly apply to Satan as well.

28:2. TO THE PRINCE OF TYRE: Since the word "prince" is sometimes used to mean "king" (see Ezekiel 37:24–25), the "prince" in verse 2 is the "king" in verse 12: Ithobaal II of Tyre. The prophet Ezekiel is dealing with the spirit of Tyre, more than just the king. This prophecy is dated shortly before the siege of Tyre by Nebuchadnezzar (585–573 BC).

I AM A GOD: Many ancient kings claimed to be gods and acted as if they were (see verse 6). When this king claimed to be a god, he was displaying the same proud attitude as the serpent who promised Adam and Eve they could be like God (see Genesis 3:5).

3–5. WISER THAN DANIEL: This is said in sarcastic derision of the leader's own exaggerated claims. Here is an indicator that Daniel, who had been captive for years in Babylon, had become well known.

6–10. STRANGERS AGAINST YOU . . . ALIENS: The reference is to invading Babylonians, and later Greeks (see Ezekiel 26). God was the true executioner.

11–19. LAMENTATION FOR THE KING OF TYRE: The lament over "the king of Tyre" now reaches behind to the real supernatural source of wickedness: Satan.

(See Matthew 16:21–23, where Peter was rebuked by the Lord as being under satanic control and motivation.)

12. THE SEAL OF PERFECTION: The Lord led Ezekiel to address the king as the one to be judged, but clearly, the power behind him was Satan. This phrase must be associated with Satan as one who was perfect in angelic beauty before he rebelled against God. But it can also relate to "perfection" in the same context of Tyre's enterprise, topmost in its trade to the ancient world (see Ezekiel 27:3–4, 11), glorious in her seafaring efforts (see 27:24), and the crowning city (see Isaiah 23:8). She is "perfect" as Jerusalem also is said to be (see 16:14; Lamentations 2:15).

FULL OF WISDOM: This refers to Satan's wisdom as an angel and to Tyre's wisdom (skill) in trade (see Ezekiel 27:8–9; 28:4).

13. YOU WERE IN EDEN: This could refer to Satan in the Garden of Eden (see Genesis 3:1–15), or it might refer to Tyre's king in a beautiful environment, a kind of Eden.

EVERY PRECIOUS STONE: This depicts Satan's rich investiture (see Genesis 2:12) and/or Tyre's king possessing every beautiful stone as Solomon had (see 1 Kings 10:10).

WORKMANSHIP OF YOUR TIMBRELS: This could refer both to Satan's once being in charge of heavenly praise and to Tyre's beautiful musical instruments used in celebration (see Ezekiel 26:13).

YOU WERE CREATED: Satan, however, is more likely to have had such wealth and beauty, wisdom, and perfection at his creation than this earthly king would have had at his birth.

14. ANOINTED CHERUB: This refers to Satan in his exalted privilege as an angel guarding (or "covering") God's throne, just as cherubim guarded Eden (see Genesis 3:24). Satan originally had continuous and unrestricted access to the glorious presence of God.

I ESTABLISHED YOU: This was true of both Satan, by God's sovereign permission, and Tyre's king.

YOU WERE ON THE HOLY MOUNTAIN: A high privilege is meant, whether referring to Satan before God in His kingdom ("the holy mountain"; see also Daniel 2:35) or to Tyre's monarch described in a picturesque analogy, as Assyria can be described as a cedar in Lebanon (see Ezekiel 31:3) to convey a picture of towering height.

15. PERFECT IN YOUR WAYS: This verse was not completely true of the king, but it was accurate of Satan before he sinned.

TILL INIQUITY WAS FOUND IN YOU: Satan's sin of pride (see Isaiah 14:14; 1 Timothy 3:6) is in view here.

16. FILLED WITH VIOLENCE: The description transitions to feature the king of Tyre, describing his demise as he followed the pattern of Satan himself.

17–19. I LAID YOU BEFORE KINGS: It would be difficult to relate this to Satan. The earthly king of Tyre, in his downfall, would be knocked or "cast" to the ground, cut down, and would lie before the gaze of other kings. From Isaiah 23:17, there is the implication of a revival under Persian rule (see Nehemiah 13:16). Two hundred and fifty years after Nebuchadnezzar, Tyre was strong enough to hold off Alexander for seven years. The Romans made it a capital of the province. Gradually, it disappeared, and its location today is not prominent.

> PROCLAMATION AGAINST SIDON: *Ezekiel describes God's judgments against Sidon, which was a sister seaport to Tyre in Phoenicia.*

21. SIDON: Sidon was located twenty-three miles north of Tyre. Even during the time of the judges (see Judges 10:6), the corrupting influence of this place had begun. It was the headquarters for Baal worship.

22–23. I EXECUTE JUDGMENTS IN HER: God would bring bloodshed and pestilence on the people there, probably at the time when He brought an invasion against Tyre.

24. NO LONGER . . . A PRICKING BRIER: This is a summary of the judgment scenarios so far revealed (Ezekiel 25–28). The enemies of Israel would be so devastated by God that (1) they would no longer be pestering Israel, and (2) they would see that the God who judges them is the true God of Israel.

25–26. WHEN I HAVE GATHERED: In this brief excursus of hope, God promised to restore Israel to the land of Palestine (see Ezekiel 34; 36–39; Isaiah 65:21; Jeremiah 30–33; Amos 9:14–15). This looks to the Messiah's earthly kingdom.

> PROCLAMATION AGAINST EGYPT: *This judgment against the powerful nation of Egypt looks ahead to 570 BC, when the Greeks of Cyrene defeated Pharaoh (Apries) Hophra, and 568/567 BC, when the Babylonians conquered Egypt.*

29:1. THE TENTH YEAR: 587 BC is the tenth year after Jehoiachin's deportation. It was one year and two days after Nebuchadnezzar had come to Jerusalem (see Ezekiel 24:1–2; 2 Kings 25:1) and seven months before its destruction (see 2 Kings 25:3–8). This is the first of seven oracles against the nation of Egypt (see Ezekiel 29:17; 30:1; 32:1; 32:17).

2. AGAINST PHARAOH . . . AGAINST ALL EGYPT: Egypt was to fall, even though it could be pictured as a water monster (see verses 3–5), a towering tree like Assyria (see 31:3), a young lion (see 32:2), and a sea monster (see 32:2–8). (See also Isaiah 19; Jeremiah 46:1–26.)

3. GREAT MONSTER: Most likely, the crocodile is the figure used for the king. Crocodiles were worshiped by the Egyptians and lived in their rivers. "Rahab" was also a general term used for a monster that often symbolized Egypt (see Psalms 87:4; 89:10; Isaiah 30:7).

4. THE FISH OF YOUR RIVERS: This figuratively represents the people who followed Pharaoh and who were a part of God's judgment on Egypt as a whole (see verses 5–6a).

6. A STAFF OF REED: The Israelites had depended on Egyptians in military alliances in the same manner as people lean on a staff that gives way, failing them. Egypt had betrayed the confidence of Israel, just as God said they would (see Jeremiah 17:5, 7). However, just because Israel never should have trusted Egypt does not lessen Egypt's judgment.

9. THE RIVER: The Nile River was the water supply for all Egypt's crops.

10. FROM MIGDOL TO SYENE: This distance covered the entirety of Egypt, since Migdol (see Exodus 14:2) was in the north and Syene in the southern border of Ethiopia.

11–12. UNINHABITED FORTY YEARS: Although it is difficult to pinpoint this time reference, one possibility is that it refers to when Babylon, under Nebuchadnezzar, reigned supreme in Egypt (see verses 19–20), from c. 568/567 BC to c. 527 BC, until Cyrus gained Persian control.

13–16. I WILL GATHER THE EGYPTIANS: Egypt regained normalcy, as is currently true, but never again reached the pinnacle of international prominence that she once enjoyed.

17. THE TWENTY-SEVENTH YEAR: This is 571/570 BC, as counted from the captivity of Jehoiachin in 597 BC, about seventeen years after the prophecy given in verses 1–16.

18. LABOR . . . AGAINST TYRE: In c. 585–573 BC, Nebuchadnezzar besieged Tyre for thirteen years before subduing the city (see Ezekiel 26:1–28:19). The Tyrians retreated to an island bastion out in the Mediterranean Sea and survived, not giving the Babylonians full satisfaction in their acquired spoils ("wages"), which would be expected after such a long struggle.

19. I WILL GIVE THE LAND OF EGYPT: To make up for Babylon's lack of sufficient reward from Tyre, God allowed a Babylonian conquest of Egypt in 568/567 BC. Babylon's army had worked as an instrument God used to bring down Egypt.

21. I WILL CAUSE THE HORN ... TO SPRING FORTH: See Ezekiel 23:25–26. God caused Israel's power to return and restored her authority as the power in an animal's horn (see 1 Samuel 2:1). Although other nations subdued her, Israel's latter end in messianic times will be blessed.

I WILL OPEN YOUR MOUTH TO SPEAK: Most likely, this refers to the day when Ezekiel's writings would be understood by looking back at their fulfillment. His muteness had already ceased in 586/585 BC when Jerusalem fell (see Ezekiel 33:21–22).

30:3. THE DAY OF THE LORD: See note on Ezekiel 13:5. Here, God's judgment day for Egypt embraces a near fulfillment in Babylon's 568/567 invasion (see 30:10; 32:11) as well as the distant Day of the Lord in the future Tribulation period when God calls all nations to judgment (see Daniel 11:42–43).

5. ETHIOPIA, LIBYA, LYDIA: See notes on Ezekiel 27:10–11; 29:10.

CHUB: An unidentified nation, along with the "mingled people" and "men of the lands." These may have been mercenaries in Egypt's army, like the previous ones in this verse.

6. MIGDOL ... SYENE: See note on Ezekiel 29:10.

8. HELPERS: All of Egypt's alliances and their arms will be useless in the day of God's judgment.

9. TO MAKE THE CARELESS ETHIOPIANS AFRAID: Apparently, the Egyptians will flee the horrors to Ethiopia and increase that nation's fear of its own inevitable judgment.

10–11. BY THE HAND OF NEBUCHADNEZZAR: He would be God's instrument of judgment.

12. RIVERS DRY: Apart from the Nile and its branches, Egypt was a barren desert. Her life depended on annual inundation of the land by the flooding Nile.

14. PATHROS: The large region south of Memphis.

ZOAN: This key city of the Nile delta's eastern portion was called Tanis by the Greeks.

15. SIN: The name referred to ancient Pelusium, a key city at the tip of the Nile River's eastern arm near the Mediterranean Sea. Given that (1) "No" (Thebes)

and "Sin" were at opposite borders of Egypt, and (2) so many cities are named, the passage speaks of judgment on the entire land.

17. AVEN: Ancient Heliopolis.

PI BESETH: The city was on the northeast branch of the Nile River where cats were mummified in honor of the cat-headed goddess, Ugastet (also called Bastet).

18. TEHAPHNEHES: This city, named after the Egyptian queen, was a residence of the pharaohs.

20. THE ELEVENTH YEAR: Circa 587/586 BC, counted from the deportation of Judah in 597 BC.

21. I HAVE BROKEN THE ARM: God figuratively depicted His act of taking power from Egypt through Nebuchadnezzar, resulting in defeat and dispersion (see verses 23, 26).

22. BREAK HIS ARMS: Both the defeat of Pharaoh Hophra (see Jeremiah 37:5ff.) and the earlier defeat of Pharaoh Necho at Carchemish (see 2 Kings 24:7; Jeremiah 46:2) are in view.

26. THEN THEY SHALL KNOW: People often don't learn that God is Lord until His judgment falls.

EGYPT CUT DOWN: Ezekiel concludes his prophecy against Egypt with an analogy comparing her to a huge tree that dominates a forest to a king/nation that dominates the world. He then offers a lamentation for both Pharaoh and the nation.

31:1. THE ELEVENTH YEAR: Circa 587/586 BC, two months after the oracle of Ezekiel 30:20-26.

2-18. WHOM ARE YOU LIKE: The prophet here reasoned that just as a strong tree "of high stature" like Assyria fell (verse 3; c. 609 BC), so will Egypt (c. 568 BC). If the Egyptians were to feel proud and invincible, they should remember how powerful Assyria had fallen already.

3. CEDAR IN LEBANON: The trees were as high as eighty feet and were an example of supreme power and domination, particularly the great cedars that grew in the mountains north of Israel.

8-9. GARDEN OF GOD . . . TREES OF EDEN: See Ezekiel 36:35; Genesis 13:10; Isaiah 51:3; Joel 2:3. Since Assyria was in the vicinity of the Garden of Eden, Ezekiel used the ultimate of gardens as a point of relative reference by which to describe tree-like Assyria.

10. BECAUSE YOU HAVE INCREASED IN HEIGHT: Ezekiel shifts from the historical illustration of Assyria's pride and fall to the reality of Egypt. God was using Assyria to teach the nations the folly of earthly power and might.

14–16. THE PIT: The scene shifts from earth and the garden of God to the grave (see Ezekiel 32:18), as God again refers to the destruction of Assyria and all her allies ("all the trees," "all that drink water").

18. WILL YOU . . . BE LIKENED: Egypt, like all the other great nations, including Assyria, will be felled by God.

32:1. THE TWELFTH YEAR: This is 585 BC, twelve years from the deportation of Judah in 597 BC.

2. LIKE A YOUNG LION: The picture here describes Egypt's deadly, energetic stalking power in her dealings with other nations. She was also violent, like the crocodile (see 29:3).

3–6. SPREAD MY NET OVER YOU: God will trap Egypt as a net snares a lion or crocodile, using many people (soldiers). The Egyptians will fall, their corpses gorging birds and beasts, their blood soaking the earth and waters.

7–8. PUT OUT YOUR LIGHT: This is likely a reference to Pharaoh, whose life and power will be extinguished, and all the rest of the leaders and people basking in his light, who will be plunged into darkness.

11–12. THE SWORD OF . . . BABYLON: This is the definite identification of the conqueror, as in Ezekiel 30:10 when Nebuchadnezzar is actually named (see also 21:19; 29:19; Jeremiah 46:26).

13–14. DESTROY ALL ITS ANIMALS: With no men or beasts to stir up the mud in the Nile River and its branches, the water will be clear and flow smoothly. Since the river was the center of all life, this pictures the devastation graphically.

17. THE TWELFTH YEAR: 585 BC, reckoned from 597 BC.

18. THE FAMOUS NATIONS: All other countries that have been conquered.

THE PIT: This refers to Sheol/the grave (see Ezekiel 31:14–16).

19–21. SPEAK TO HIM OUT OF THE MIDST OF HELL: The prophet Ezekiel follows Egypt and her people beyond the grave. The king of Egypt is addressed by the other nations as being in "hell," taunting him, as he is now on the same level with them. This shows that there is a conscious existence and a fixed destiny beyond death (see Luke 16:19–31).

22. ASSYRIA IS THERE: The slain of several nations are pictured in the afterlife: Assyria (verses 22–23), Elam (verses 24–25), Meshech and Tubal (verses 26–28; see also notes on Ezekiel 38:1–2), and Edom (verses 29–30). Although

mighty for a time on earth, the fallen lie as defeated equals in death, all conquered by God and consigned to eternal hell (see verse 21).

31–32. PHARAOH . . . COMFORTED: A strange comfort coming from the recognition that he and his people were not alone in their misery and doom.

UNLEASHING THE TEXT

1) What do you learn about Tyre as a nation and civilization from Ezekiel 26–27?

_____

_____

_____

_____

_____

_____

2) What were the reasons for God's judgment against Tyre and Sidon according to Ezekiel 28?

_____

_____

_____

_____

_____

_____

3) What images stand out to you from God's proclamation against Egypt in Ezekiel 29–30? What do they explain?

_____

_____

_____

_____

_____

_____

_____

4) What is the significance of God comparing Egypt to a great tree in Ezekiel 31? What did God say would happen to this "strong tree" among the nations?

_____

_____

_____

_____

_____

_____

_____

EXPLORING THE MEANING

Do not put your trust in worldly wealth. Tyre was not as infamous an enemy of Israel as were Egypt and Edom. In fact, Tyre had been a friend to Israel during the time of David and Solomon, even providing the cedar lumber for the temple (see 1 Kings 5). Yet the people of Tyre stirred up God's wrath through their idolatry and evil practices. When we look at the lamentation for Tyre in Ezekiel 27, it is clear the nation possessed great wealth. They were the "merchant of the peoples on many coastlands" (verse 3). They had a fleet of lovely and effective ships that exchanged goods from all over the world. They trafficked in "luxury goods" (verse 12), including precious metals, horses, ivory, embroidery, fine linen, and even corals. Yet the presence of that wealth and industry could not protect them from God's judgment: "You enriched the kings of the earth with your many luxury goods and your merchandise. But you are broken by the seas in the depths of the waters" (verses 33–34). As Jesus would later say, "No one can serve two masters. . . . You cannot serve God and mammon" (Matthew 6:24).

Do not put your trust in worldly might. In Ezekiel 29, God turned His attention to Egypt. The opening of that chapter is attention-grabbing to say the least: "Behold, I am against you, O Pharaoh king of Egypt, O great monster who lies in the midst of his rivers, who has said, 'My River is my own; I have made it for myself.' But I will put hooks in your jaws . . . I will bring you up out of the midst of your rivers" (verses 3–4). The connection between Egypt and a crocodile was a representation of that nation's great military strength. (It was also significant because crocodiles were one of the false gods worshiped by the Egyptian people.) However, later in that same chapter, God described Egypt as "a staff of reed to the house of Israel" (verse 6). Israel had leaned on the Egyptians in military alliances like a person leans on a staff. But when that staff "of reed" broke, Judah was even more vulnerable than before. As David wrote, "Some trust in chariots, and some in horses; but we will remember the name of the LORD" (Psalm 20:7).

Do not put your trust in anything of this world. In Ezekiel 28, God directed His prophet to describe the king of Tyre using language and imagery that can also be connected to Satan. For instance, in one place Ezekiel writes of the king, "You were the seal of perfection, full of wisdom and perfect in beauty. You were in Eden, the garden of God" (verses 12–13). Similarly, he writes, "You were the anointed cherub who covers; I established you; you were on the holy mountain of God" (verse 14). By making a direct link between Satan and the king of Tyre—a pagan and rebellious nation—God was revealing Satan to be the power behind that king. Satan had fueled the rise of Tyre as an enemy of God's people and had directly influenced her king to thwart God's plans. Importantly, the descriptions in Ezekiel 28:1–19 *do* apply to the human person who ruled as the king of Tyre and are not allegorical. However, these verses contain multiple layers in that they also highlight Satan's influence in the lives of all people who choose to make themselves an enemy of God. In the end, all the plans of such people will fail (see Psalm 37:12–15), just as all the plans of Satan will ultimately come to destruction.

REFLECTING ON THE TEXT

5)   Why do so many people put their trust in wealth, power, and resources instead of God? Where do you see people relying on worldly philosophies and ideologies rather than God's Word?

_____

_____

_____

_____

_____

_____

_____

_____

_____

6) What is the danger in putting your trust in the might of human institutions (like governments and organizations) instead of in God?

_____

_____

_____

_____

_____

_____

_____

_____

7) How does the Bible describe the role and activity of Satan in human affairs? According to Scripture, what influence or power does he have on people in the world today?

_____

_____

_____

_____

_____

_____

_____

_____

8) Paul wrote that Jesus "disarmed principalities and powers . . . triumphing over them" (Colossians 2:15). What does this say about the fate of all Satan's schemes?

_____

_____

_____

_____

_____

_____

_____

PERSONAL RESPONSE

9) Where are you currently placing your trust in something other than God (whether it is wealth, power, resources, relationships, or anything else)?

_____

_____

_____

_____

_____

_____

_____

10) What are Satan's strategies to deceive and tempt us? What strategies does the Bible describe for resisting those attacks?

_____

_____

_____

_____

_____

_____

8

REGATHERING IN THE LAND
Ezekiel 33:1–36:38

DRAWING NEAR

What does the Bible have to say about future hope for believers? What are some of the things that God has promised to those who are faithful to Him?

_____

_____

_____

_____

_____

_____

_____

_____

_____

_____

_____

_____

THE CONTEXT

Let's take a moment to review the structure of Ezekiel's book so far. The opening chapters (1–3) describe God's personal call to Ezekiel to serve as His prophet and to speak His words to the stiff-necked people of Judah. Chapters 4–24 include a series of prophetic words, visions, and object lessons delivered by

Ezekiel to proclaim God's intention to destroy His holy city and even His temple through the "sword of Babylon." These chapters were addressed primarily to the captives of Judah living with Ezekiel—captives who were confident that Jerusalem would be saved and they would return to the promised land. Chapters 25–32 then offer proclamations of judgment against seven other nations who had also rebelled against God.

As we will uncover in this session, chapter 33 serves as a transition between the first half of Ezekiel's prophetic record and the second. This transition represents the historical moment of Jerusalem's fall and the destruction of the temple—news that Ezekiel and the other captives learned from a survivor (or survivors) who made it all the way to Babylon.

Chapter 34 represents the start of another series of prophecies that continues through chapter 48. In these messages, Ezekiel's primary theme is the future restoration of Israel, Judah, and Jerusalem. In other words, these prophecies from Ezekiel primarily offer hope to the people rather than judgment. They emphasize God's grace and mercy and point forward to a future regathering of God's people in their promised land. For that reason, many of the prophecies in this section have strong connections to the Millennium.

KEYS TO THE TEXT

Read Ezekiel 33:1–36:38, noting the key words and phrases indicated below.

> *THE WATCHMAN AND HIS MESSAGE: Ezekiel 33 serves as a transition between God's judgments against Jerusalem and the nations (chapters 1–32) and Israel's bright future when she is restored to her land (chapters 34–48).*

33:1. AGAIN THE WORD OF THE LORD CAME TO ME: Ezekiel will now provide God's instructions for national repentance. This chapter serves as the preface to the prophecies of comfort and salvation that will follow in chapters 34–39.

2. SPEAK TO THE CHILDREN OF YOUR PEOPLE: This was given to prepare the exiles' minds to look on the awful calamity in Jerusalem as a just act by God (see Ezekiel 14:21–23). The Lord had faithfully warned them, but they had not heeded that warning. Ezekiel had been forbidden to speak to his people from the time he references in 24:26–27 until Jerusalem was captured. Meanwhile, he had spoken to the foreign nations (chapters 25–32).

2–9. WATCHMAN: Men such as Jeremiah and Ezekiel (see 3:16–21) were spiritual watchmen (33:7–9), warning that God would bring a sword on His people so they had the opportunity to prepare and be safe. This analogy came from the custom of putting guards on the city wall watching for the approach of danger, and then trumpeting the warning. For the function of a watchman, see 2 Samuel 18:24–25; 2 Kings 9:17; Jeremiah 4:5; 6:1; Hosea 8:1; Amos 3:6; Habakkuk 2:1. (See also the notes on Ezekiel 3:17–21.)

4. HIS BLOOD . . . ON HIS OWN HEAD: Once the watchman did his duty, the responsibility passed to each person. (See the notes on Ezekiel 18, where each person is accountable for his own response to God's warnings, whether to die in judgment or to live as one who heeded and repented.) Ezekiel had been a very faithful and obedient watchman.

8–9. HIS BLOOD I WILL REQUIRE: A prophet who sounded the warning of repentance for sin was not to be judged (verse 9), but the one who failed to deliver the message was held accountable (verse 8). This referred to unfaithfulness on the part of the prophet, for which he bore responsibility and was chastened by God (see Acts 20:26).

10–11. HOW CAN WE THEN LIVE: The Israelites reasoned that if they were liable to death in judgment that was inevitable, they were in a hopeless condition and had no future. God replied that He had no pleasure in seeing the wicked die for their sin but desired them to repent and live (see 2 Peter 3:9). The divine answer to the human question—"how can we then live?"—is "repent and be saved!" (see Ezekiel 18:23, 30–32). Here was a blending of divine compassion with the demands of God's holiness. Repentance and forgiveness were offered to all.

12–20. THE RIGHTEOUSNESS OF THE RIGHTEOUS MAN SHALL NOT DELIVER HIM: See notes on Ezekiel 18:19–29. One of the basic principles of God's dealing with His people is presented here: judgment is according to personal faith and conduct. The discussion is not about eternal salvation and eternal death but physical death as judgment for sin, which, for believers, could not result in eternal death. The righteous behavior in verse 15 could only characterize a true believer, who was faithful from the heart. There is no distinction made in the matter of who is a true believer in God. There is only a discussion of the issue of behavior as a factor in physical death. For those who were apostate idolaters, physical death would lead to eternal death. For believers who were lovers of the true God, their sin would lead only to physical punishment (see 1 Corinthians 11:28–31; 1 John 5:16–17). "Righteous" and "wicked" are terms describing behavior, not a person's position before God. It is not the "righteousness of God" imputed as illustrated in the case of Abraham (see Genesis 15:6; Romans 4:3–5), but rather one's deeds that are in view (verses 15–19).

17, 20. NOT FAIR: The people blamed God for their calamities, when actually they were being judged for their sins.

21. THE CITY HAS BEEN CAPTURED: A fugitive or fugitives (the Hebrew could be a collective noun) who escaped from Jerusalem reached Ezekiel with this report on January 8, 585 BC, almost six months after the fall of the city on July 18, 586 (see Jeremiah 39:1–2; 52:5–7). Based on Ezekiel 24:1–2 and 33:21, there was a thirty-six month span from the outset of the siege of the city on January 15, 588, to when Ezekiel received the report.

22. OPENED MY MOUTH: God exercised control over the mouth of Ezekiel (see note on 3:26–27).

23–29. THEN THE WORD OF THE LORD CAME TO ME: There is no date attached to the prophecies from Ezekiel 33:23–39:29, but the first message after the fall of Jerusalem was a rebuke of Israel's carnal confidence. This prophecy was against the remnant of Judah who remained in the land of promise after the fall of Jerusalem. Ezekiel warns these survivors that more judgment will come on them if they do not obey God. By some strange reasoning, they thought that if God had given the land to Abraham when he was alone, it would be more securely theirs because they were many in number—a claim based on quantity rather than quality (verse 24). But judgment would come if they turned and rejected God again (verses 25–29).

30–33. THEY HEAR YOUR WORDS, BUT THEY DO NOT DO THEM: Here was a message to exiles, who had no intention of obeying the prophet's messages. They liked to listen but not apply the prophet's words. They finally knew, by bitter experience, that he had spoken the truth of God. The people appreciated the eloquence of Ezekiel but not the reality of his message.

A TRUE SHEPHERD: Ezekiel's messages now become mostly comforting, telling of God's grace and faithfulness to His covenant promises.

34:2–4. PROPHESY AGAINST THE SHEPHERDS: The reference is to preexilic leaders such as kings, priests, and prophets—that is, the false leaders who fleeced the flock for personal gain (verses 3–4), rather than the true leaders who fed or led righteously (as in Ezekiel 22:25–28; Jeremiah 14, 23; Zechariah 11). This stands in contrast to the Lord as Shepherd in Psalms 23; 80:1; Isaiah 40:11; Jeremiah 31:10; Luke 15:4–5; John 10:1ff.

5. FOOD FOR ALL THE BEASTS: The beasts pictured nations that prey on Israel (see Daniel 7:3–7), though it could possibly include actual wild beasts, as in Ezekiel 14:21. (See notes on 34:25, 28–29.)

9–10. CAUSE THEM TO CEASE FEEDING THE SHEEP: This was no idle threat, as proven by the case of King Zedekiah (see Jeremiah 52:10–11).

11. I MYSELF WILL SEARCH: God, the true Shepherd, would search out and find His sheep in order to restore Israel to their land, for the kingdom the Messiah will lead (see verses 12–14).

12. A CLOUDY AND DARK DAY: This refers to the Day of the Lord judgment on Israel (see Jeremiah 30:4–7).

12–14. I WILL . . . GATHER THEM: Here is the promise of a literal regathering and restoration of the people of Israel to their land from their worldwide dispersion. Since the scattering was literal, the regathering must also be literal. Once they are regathered in the Messiah's kingdom, they will not lack anything.

15–16. I WILL FEED MY FLOCK: In contrast to the self-indulgent leaders who took advantage of the sheep, God will meet the needs of His sheep (people). This is clearly reminiscent of Psalm 23 and will be fulfilled by the Good Shepherd (see John 10:1ff.), who will reign as Israel's shepherd.

17–22. JUDGE BETWEEN: Once God has judged the leaders, He will also judge the abusive members of the flock as to their true spiritual state. This passage anticipates the judgment of the people given by Jesus Christ in Matthew 25:31–46. The ungodly are known because they trample the poor. The Lord alone is able to sort out the true from the false (see the parables of Matthew 13) and will do so in the final kingdom.

23. ONE SHEPHERD . . . DAVID: This refers to the greater One in David's dynasty (see 2 Samuel 7:12–16), the Messiah, who will be Israel's ultimate king over the millennial kingdom (see Jeremiah 30:9; Hosea 3:5; Zechariah 14:9).

24. THE LORD: This is God the Father.

A PRINCE. The word can at times be used of the king himself (see Ezekiel 37:34–35; 28:2, 12), as is the case here.

25. A COVENANT OF PEACE: This refers to the New Covenant of Jeremiah 31:31–34 in full operation during the millennial kingdom.

WILD BEASTS: This refers to actual animals that will be tamed in the kingdom (see Isaiah 11:6–9; 35:9; Hosea 2:18).

26. MY HILL: A reference to Jerusalem and Zion in particular, where the Jews will come to worship the Lord.

SHOWERS OF BLESSING: See the "times of refreshing" in Acts 3:19–20, when the curses of Deuteronomy 28:15–68 are lifted.

27. SHALL YIELD THEIR FRUIT: The faithfulness of the land is also indicated in Amos 9:13.

28–29. NO LONGER BE A PREY: God will stop other nations from subjugating the people of Israel.

30. I, THE LORD THEIR GOD: An often-repeated Old Testament theme (see Genesis 17:7–8), this phrase speaks of the ultimate salvation of Israel (as in Romans 11:25–27).

> JUDGMENT ON MOUNT SEIR: *Ezekiel now describes God's judgment against "Mount Seir," another name for Edom, and prophesizes the disaster that will come to her. The Edomites represented Israel's most inveterate and bitter enemy.*

35:2. AGAINST MOUNT SEIR: The Edomites were also threatened with judgment in Ezekiel 25:12–14. The land of Edom was located east of the Arabah from the Dead Sea to the Gulf of Aqaba. The main cities were Teman and Petra, which are now in ruins.

3–4. I WILL STRETCH OUT MY LAND: This prediction (see verses 6–9) came to pass literally, first by Nebuchadnezzar (sixth century BC) and later by John Hyrcanus (126 BC). There is no trace of the Edomites now, though their desolate cities can be identified, as predicted by Obadiah (see Obadiah 1:18) and Jeremiah (see Jeremiah 49:13).

5. BECAUSE: God will judge Edom because of (1) her perpetual enmity against Israel since Esau's hatred of Jacob (see Genesis 25–28), and (2) Edom's spiteful bloodshed against the Israelites trying to escape the Babylonians in 586 BC.

10. BECAUSE: A further reason for Edom's doom was her design to take control of the territory occupied by "two nations"; that is, Israel (north) and Judah (south). The Edomites plotted to take over these nations for their own gain (see verse 12) but were prevented from doing this and subsequently destroyed because "the LORD was there."

11–12. ANGER . . . ENVY . . . BLASPHEMIES: Here were more reasons for Edom's destruction.

13. YOU . . . BOASTED AGAINST ME: Still another reason for judgment was Edom's proud ambitions that were really against God (see verse 10, "although the LORD was there").

15. AS YOU REJOICED: This final reason for the Edomites' doom was their joy over Israel's calamity.

THEY SHALL KNOW: The ultimate aim in Edom's judgment was so "the whole earth" would know that the Lord is God and see His glory. Sadly, sinners find this out only in their own destruction (see Hebrews 10:31).

36:1. AND YOU, SON OF MAN, PROPHESY: This chapter presents the prerequisite regeneration that Israel must experience before they can nationally enter into the promised blessings. This chapter must be understood to speak of a literal Israel, a literal land, and a literal regeneration, leading to a literal kingdom under the Messiah.

TO THE MOUNTAINS: Ezekiel addresses Israel's mountains, as symbolic of the whole nation (see verses 1, 4, 6, 8). God promises: (1) to give these mountains again to dispersed Israel (verse 12), (2) to cause fruit to grow on them (verse 8), (3) to rebuild cities and multiply the people there (verse 10), and (4) to bless in a greater way than in the past (verse 11). These promises can only be fulfilled in future millennial blessings to Israel that she has not yet experienced, because they include the salvation of the New Covenant (see verses 25–27, 29, 31, 33).

2. BECAUSE THE ENEMY HAS SAID: This section (through verse 15) continues the prophecy against Edom from Ezekiel 35. God will restore the "ancient heights" to Israel, which their enemies claimed to possess (see Genesis 12:7). They will pay for their spite against Israel.

7. RAISED MY HAND IN AN OATH: God testifies, as a formal pledge, that He will bring a turnabout in which the nations that seized the land will be shamed.

BLESSING ON ISRAEL: Ezekiel now relates God's blessing on His people, elaborating on how Israel's land will again be productive, populated, and peaceful.

8–15. YIELD YOUR FRUIT . . . MULTIPLY MEN . . . DEVOUR MEN NO MORE: These features of Israel's land—productive (verses 8–9), populated (verses 10–11), and peaceful (verses 12–15)—will be fully realized in the Messiah's kingdom. The people's return from Babylon was only a partial fulfillment and foreshadowing of the fullness to come in the future kingdom.

16–19. DEFILED IT: Ezekiel gives a backward look to underscore why Israel had suffered past judgments by the Lord. It was because the Jews had "defiled" their land by their sins that the Lord purged it. He likened such a defilement to a menstrual condition (verse 17).

20. THEY PROFANED MY HOLY NAME: Even in dispersion, the Israelites tainted God's honor in the sight of the heathen, who concluded that the Lord of this exiled people was not powerful enough to keep them in their land.

21–23. FOR MY HOLY NAME'S SAKE: Restoring Israel to the land that God pledged in covenant (see Genesis 12:7) will sanctify His great name and move other peoples to "know that I am the LORD." This glory for God is the primary reason for Israel's restoration (see verse 32).

24. INTO YOUR OWN LAND: God assured Israel that He will bring them out of other lands back to the promised land, the very land from which He scattered them (see verse 20). This is the same "land that I gave to your fathers" (verse 28), a land distinct from those of other nations (see verse 36), and a land whose cities will be inhabited by those who return (see verses 33, 36, 38). The establishment of the modern state of Israel indicates this has initially begun.

25–31. SPRINKLE CLEAN WATER ON YOU: This section is among the most glorious in Scripture on the subject of Israel's restoration to God and national salvation. This salvation is described in verse 25 as a cleansing that will wash away sin. Such washing was symbolized in the Mosaic rites of purification (see Numbers 19:17–19; Psalm 119:9; Isaiah 4:4; Zechariah 13:1; for the concept of sprinkling in cleansing, see Psalm 51:7, 10; Hebrews 9:13; 10:22). Paul wrote of this washing in Ephesians 5:26 and Titus 3:5. Jesus had this very promise in mind in John 3:5.

25. I WILL CLEANSE YOU: Along with the physical reality of a return to the land, God pledged spiritual renewal that included: (1) cleansing from sin, (2) a new heart of the New Covenant (see Jeremiah 31:31–34), (3) a new spirit or disposition inclined to worship Him, and (4) His Spirit dwelling in them, enabling them to walk in obedience to His word. This has not happened, because Israel has not trusted Jesus Christ as Messiah and Savior, but it will before the kingdom of the Messiah (see Zechariah 12–14; Romans 11:25–27; Revelation 11:13).

26–27. I WILL GIVE YOU A NEW HEART . . . NEW SPIRIT: What was figuratively described in verse 25 is explained as literal in verses 26 and 27. The gift of the "new heart" signifies the new birth, which is regeneration by the Holy Spirit (see Ezekiel 11:18–20). The "heart" stands for the whole nature. The "spirit" indicates the governing power of the mind, which directs thought and conduct.

A "stony heart" is stubborn and self-willed. A "heart of flesh" is pliable and responsive. The evil inclination is removed and a new nature replaces it. This is New Covenant character, as in Jeremiah 31:31–34.

27–30. MY SPIRIT: God will also give His "Spirit" to the faithful Jews (see Ezekiel 39:29; Isaiah 44:3; 59:21; Joel 2:28–29; Acts 2:16ff.). When Israel becomes the true people of God (verse 28), the judgment promise of Hosea 1:9 will be nullified. All nature will experience the blessings of Israel's salvation (verses 29–30).

31–32. YOU WILL REMEMBER YOUR EVIL WAYS: When the Jews have experienced such grace, they will be even more repentant—a sign of true conversion. Ezekiel thus profoundly proclaims the doctrines of conversion and spiritual life. He includes forgiveness (verse 25), regeneration (verse 26), the indwelling Holy Spirit (verse 27), and responsive obedience to God's law (verse 27). These are all presented as he prophesizes Israel's conversion. As a nation, they will know their God (verse 38), hate their sin (verses 31–32), and glorify their Savior (verse 32).

32. NOT FOR YOUR SAKE: God's glory and reputation among the nations, not Israel's, causes this restoration to be promised (see Psalm 115:1; Acts 5:41; Romans 1:5; 3 John 1:7).

35. THE GARDEN: Millennial conditions will be similar (though not identical) to those in Eden (see Ezekiel 47:1–12; Isaiah 35:1–2; 55:13; Zechariah 8:12).

37. INQUIRE OF ME TO DO THIS: God will sovereignly work this return/renewal yet give Israelites the human privilege of praying for it to be realized. This prophecy was intended to stir up the people's prayers.

37–38. INCREASE THEIR MEN: There will be an increase in the population during the Millennium. When the male population came to Jerusalem, they brought vast numbers of animals for sacrifice, but that was small compared to future kingdom conditions.

UNLEASHING THE TEXT

1) What was Ezekiel's role as a "watchman" (see Ezekiel 33)? How had he fulfilled this role?

_____

_____

_____

_____

_____

_____

2) Look at Ezekiel 34:11–31. How do these verses point to Jesus the Messiah?

_____

_____

_____

_____

3) What do those verses say about God's care for His people as their shepherd?

_____

_____

_____

_____

4) What promise does God give to His people in Ezekiel 36:24–32?

_____

_____

_____

_____

EXPLORING THE MEANING

God desires His people to live and thrive. Ezekiel's prophecies about the judgment of Judah and destruction of Jerusalem could cause some to conclude that God duplicitously wanted to destroy His people. There are certainly those who picture God as an angry deity looking for a reason to send thunderbolts against people in the world. Of course, this is not the case. Ezekiel's prophecies and visions were part of God's attempt to warn His people about the sinful trajectory of their own lives and nation as a whole. This is why God continually sent prophets like Ezekiel to His people—to help them see the error of their ways and turn aside so they could *avoid* judgment. God clearly revealed this aspect of His character in Ezekiel 33: "'As I live,' says the Lord GOD, 'I have no pleasure in the death of the wicked, but that the wicked turn from his way and live. Turn, turn from your evil ways! For why should you die, O house of Israel?" (verse 11). For Christians today, Scripture, and those who faithfully proclaim it, serve as our "watchman," revealing what we must do in order to live and thrive as children of God.

God desires His people to repent. The crisis highlighted thus far in Ezekiel is that God's people had rejected Him and pursued the gods and lifestyles of the pagan nations. Their choices had put them on a pathway to ruin—a pathway God wanted them to avoid. He desired His people to listen to Ezekiel (and the other prophets) and *repent* of their sins. God had heard the people of Judah asking, "If our transgressions and our sins lie upon us, and we pine away in them, how can we then live?" (33:10). The Lord gave this answer through Ezekiel: "Turn, turn from your evil ways! For why should you die, O house of Israel?" (verse 11). This same pattern has been repeated throughout human history. When people seek to remain sovereign over their own lives, they steer themselves toward destruction. God's desire is to warn all people away from that destruction and for them to repent. In the words of Peter: "The Lord is not slack concerning His promise, as some count slackness, but is longsuffering toward us, not willing that any should perish but that all should come to repentance" (2 Peter 3:9).

God desires righteous leaders for His people. One of the reasons Judah continually fell into idolatry was because her leaders—including kings, priests, false prophets, and others—were largely selfish, greedy, and corrupt. Rather than leading the people as examples of righteousness, they preyed upon those within their care. God said of them, "Woe to the shepherds of Israel who feed themselves! Should not the shepherds feed the flocks? You eat the fat and clothe yourselves with the wool; you slaughter the fatlings, but you do not feed the flock" (34:2–3). God then pointed to a moment in the future when *He* would step in as the shepherd of His people: "Indeed I Myself will search for My sheep and seek them out" (verse 11), and later, "I will feed them in good pasture, and their fold shall be on the high mountains of Israel. There they shall lie down in a good fold and feed in rich pasture" (verse 14). These verses point forward to the coming of Jesus as the Good Shepherd who would lay down His life for the sheep (see John 10:11). They also point forward to the millennial kingdom, when God's people will receive blessing upon blessing in a restored Israel.

REFLECTING ON THE TEXT

5) How has God's Word served as a "watchman" to help you guard against sin?

_____

_____

_____

_____

_____

6) What does it mean to repent? According to Scripture, what does repentance look like on a practical level?

_____

_____

_____

_____

7) Who has been an example of a godly leader in your life? What did that person do that helped you "traverse the way of righteousness"(Proverbs 8:20)?

_____

_____

_____

_____

8) Jesus said, "My sheep hear My voice, and I know them" (John 10:27). How have you seen Christ shepherd you from the time of your salvation until now?

_____

_____

_____

_____

PERSONAL RESPONSE

9) Are there any areas of your life in which you need to repent of rebellion against God? What should that repentance involve?

_____

_____

_____

_____

10) Are there any pressing areas in your life for which you ought to seek the Lord's guidance in His Word? (If so, study Scripture and pray to your loving Shepherd for wisdom in applying it.)

_____

_____

_____

_____

9

PICTURES OF RESTORATION
Ezekiel 37:1–39:29

DRAWING NEAR
Who do you know whose life was very obviously changed by the work of God in salvation? What made the transformation in that person's life so remarkable?

_____
_____
_____
_____
_____
_____
_____
_____
_____
_____
_____
_____
_____
_____
_____

THE CONTEXT
The destruction of Jerusalem was a pivotal moment in the history of God's people—one that, in spite of God's many warnings, they largely didn't believe could

happen. Remember that the Assyrians had besieged Jerusalem back in 701 BC after their conquest of Israel, the northern kingdom. This siege was broken by divine intervention (see 2 Kings 18–19). Later, Nebuchadnezzar of Babylon besieged Jerusalem in 597 BC. This was the second wave of Judah's conquest, during which time many captives were taken back to Babylon. However, while that siege resulted in Jerusalem's surrender, it did not involve the city's destruction.

For those reasons and more, both the remaining residents in Jerusalem and the captives in Babylon firmly believed that God would do something to disrupt or distract Nebuchadnezzar's second siege of the holy city in 587 and 586 BC. They were confident God would once again step in to save the city in which He caused His name to dwell. Of course, we know they were mistaken. Jerusalem's resistance was broken in 586 BC, its walls destroyed, its people killed, and its temple ravaged. Again, this was a pivotal moment in Israel's history.

Immediately after that destruction, however, God began to speak through His prophet Ezekiel about restoration. Much of that restoration is spiritual; God promised to cleanse His people from their sin: "I will give you a new heart and put a new spirit within you; I will take the heart of stone out of your flesh and give you a heart of flesh" (36:26). But much of that restoration would also be physical in the form of a new, glorified nation during the millennial reign of Christ. We will explore both of these themes in this lesson.

KEYS TO THE TEXT

Read Ezekiel 37:1–39:29, noting the key words and phrases indicated below.

> *DRY BONES AND TWO STICKS: God gives Ezekiel a vision of a valley filled with dry bones and an object lesson with two sticks to show the restoration of Israel.*

37:1. BROUGHT ME . . . IN THE SPIRIT: Ezekiel is given another vision in 37:1–14. God does not change Ezekiel's location but gives him a vivid, inward sense that he has been taken to a valley "full of bones." (For other visions, see Ezekiel 1:1–3:15; 8:1–11:24; 40:1–48:35.) This passage, part of a series of revelations received during the night before the messenger came with the news of the destruction of Jerusalem, was to ease the gloom of the people.

IN THE MIDST OF THE VALLEY: This no doubt represents the world area wherever Israelites were scattered (see verse 12).

2. VERY DRY: This language pictures the dead nation as lifeless, scattered, and bleached, just as a dry tree (see 17:24) pictures a dead nation to which only God can give life.

3. CAN THESE BONES LIVE: The many dry bones (see verse 2) picture the nation of Israel (see verse 11) as apparently dead in their dispersion and waiting for national resurrection. The people knew about the doctrine of individual resurrection; otherwise this prophecy would have had no meaning (see 1 Kings 17; 2 Kings 4; 13:21; Isaiah 25:8; 26:19; Daniel 12:2; Hosea 13:14).

4–6. PROPHESY TO THESE BONES: Ezekiel is to proclaim God's pledge to reassemble the Israelites from all over the world, restore the nation of Israel to life (see verse 5), and give them His Spirit (see verse 14) in true salvation and spiritual life. Clearly, God is promising the resurrection of Israel as a nation and its spiritual regeneration (see Ezekiel 36:25–27).

7–10. PROPHESIED AS I WAS COMMANDED: In the vision, Ezekiel did as he was told, and the dead bones became a living nation (verse 10).

11–13. THE BONES ARE THE WHOLE HOUSE OF ISRAEL: This passage contains the key to unlock the interpretation of the vision. It is the resurrection and salvation of Israel.

14. I, THE LORD . . . PERFORMED IT: God's reputation is at stake in the restoration and regeneration of Israel to the land. He must do what He promised so all will know that He is Lord.

15–23. A STICK . . . ANOTHER STICK: The vision ended, and Ezekiel was given an object lesson that his people observed (verses 18, 20). This drama of uniting two sticks offered a second illustration that God will not only regather Israelites to their land but also will, for the first time since 931 BC (the end of Solomon's reign; see 1 Kings 11:26–40), restore union between Israel and Judah (verses 19, 21–22) in the messianic reign (see Isaiah 11:12–13; Jeremiah 3:18; Hosea 1:11).

21–23. THEN SAY TO THEM: God makes three promises that summarize His future plans for Israel: (1) restoration (verse 21), (2) unification (verse 22), and (3) purification (verse 23). These promises bring to fulfillment: (1) the Abrahamic covenant (see Genesis 12); (2) the Davidic covenant (see 2 Samuel 7); and (3) the New Covenant (see Jeremiah 31), respectively.

22. ONE KING SHALL BE KING OVER THEM ALL: This leader (see verses 24–25) is the Messiah-King-Shepherd, often promised for David's dynasty (see Ezekiel 34:23–24; Jeremiah 23:5–8; 30:9; Daniel 2:35, 45; 7:13–14, 27), who is the one king of Zechariah 14:9 (see also Matthew 25:31, 34, 40).

23. CLEANSE THEM: This is provided by the provisions of the New Covenant (see Ezekiel 36:27; 37:14; Jeremiah 31:31–34).

24–25. DAVID: This is to be understood as Jesus Christ the Messiah, descendant of David (see 2 Samuel 7:8–17; Isaiah 7:14; 9:6–7; Micah 5:2; Matthew 1:1, 23; Luke 1:31–33).

25. LAND THAT I HAVE GIVEN TO JACOB: It is natural to see this physical land, so clarified, as the very land God gave to Abraham, Isaac, and Jacob (see Genesis 12:7; 26:24; 35:12).

26. COVENANT OF PEACE: See Ezekiel 34:25. This is the New Covenant in full force. Israel has never yet been in a state of perpetual salvation peace, so this awaits fulfillment in the future kingdom of the Messiah, who is the Prince of Peace (see Isaiah 9:6).

AN EVERLASTING COVENANT: The everlasting nature of the Abrahamic (Genesis 17:7), Davidic (2 Samuel 23:5), and New (Jeremiah 50:5) Covenants are joined together in the redeemed who experience the millennial kingdom "forever" (used four times in verses 25–28). The Hebrew word for "everlasting" may refer to a long time or to eternity. It is also true that these covenants will continue to be fulfilled after the Millennium in the eternal state.

MY SANCTUARY: The Spirit of God begins to prepare for the great reality that God will have a sanctuary in the midst of His people and will dwell with them (see Zechariah 6:12–13). God promised to dwell with man on earth (see Ezekiel 47:1–12). This has been God's desire in all epochs: (1) before Moses (see Genesis 17:7–8), (2) in the Mosaic era (see Leviticus 26:11–13), (3) in the church era (see 1 Corinthians 3:16; 6:19), (4) in the Millennium (see Ezekiel 37:26–28), and (5) in eternity future (see Revelation 21:3).

27. I WILL BE THEIR GOD: Paul quotes this text in 2 Corinthians 6:16.

GOG AND ALLIES ATTACK ISRAEL: *Ezekiel's next prophecy from the Lord tells of a coming northern confederacy of nations that will invade the promised land.*

38:2. GOG: This name is found in 1 Chronicles 5:4. The Septuagint used Gog to render names such as Agag (see Numbers 24:7) and Og (see Deuteronomy 3:1), possibly showing that though it was a proper name, it came to be used as a general title for an enemy of God's people. Gog most likely carries the idea of "high" or "supreme one," based on the comparison in Numbers 24:7. It refers to a person, described as a "prince" from the land of Magog, who is the final Antichrist. Gog and Magog are referred to again in Revelation 20:8, where the titles are used symbolically of the final world uprising against Jerusalem, its people, and Messiah King. This attack comes not just from the north but from the four corners of the world, as a world of sinners at the end of the thousand-year kingdom come to fight the saints in the "beloved city" of Jerusalem. On that occasion, there is only one weapon used—divine fire. This is the climax to the last battle with Satan and his armies, whose eternal destiny is set. It is followed by the final judgment of all the ungodly before the Lord (see Revelation 20:11–15) and the creation of the eternal, sinless state (see 21:1). (See also notes on Ezekiel 39.)

MAGOG: Some see this people as derived from Japheth (see Genesis 10:2), later called the Scythians. Others propose a people in southeast Anatolia, later known as peoples such as the Mongols and Huns. Others see Magog as an overall term for barbarians, north of Palestine, around the Caspian and Black Seas.

THE PRINCE OF ROSH, MESHECH, AND TUBAL: This should be translated "chief prince of Meshech and Tubal" because: (1) Rosh (more than 600 times) in the Hebrew Old Testament is an adjective, "chief," often used in reference to the "chief priest" (see 2 Kings 25:18); (2) most ancient versions took Rosh to mean "chief " or "head"; and (3) in all places other than Ezekiel 38 and 39, where both Meshech and Tubal are mentioned, Rosh is not listed as a third people (see Ezekiel 27:13; 32:26; Genesis 10:2; 1 Chronicles 1:5). This is also descriptive of the Antichrist, who will rise to world dominance during the coming time of Tribulation (see Daniel 9:24–27; 11:36–45; Revelation 13:1–17; 19:20).

MESHECH, AND TUBAL: Two people groups were recognized on ancient Assyrian monuments: one called Mushki (Mushku) and the other Tubali (Tabal). Both were in Asia Minor, the area of Magog, modern-day Turkey. In summary, a chief prince, who is the enemy of God's people, will lead a coalition of nations against Jerusalem. The details of this enemy force and its destruction are given by Ezekiel in the rest of chapters 38 and 39.

4. I WILL . . . LEAD YOU OUT: God aims to use this army as human invaders for His judgments, just as He used Assyria (see Isaiah 8) and Babylon (see Ezekiel 21:19). In this case, God brings the invader to Palestine so that He may visit judgment (see verse 8) on the invader itself (see 38:18–23; 39:1–10). Ezekiel thus uses the language of "hooks into your jaws," just as was used in the judgment against Egypt (see 29:4). From the aggressors' perspective, they think it is their plan only to seize the spoil that draws them to Palestine (see 38:11–12).

5. PERSIA, ETHIOPIA, AND LIBYA: The invasion involves a coalition of powers from the east and south of Palestine. Persia is modern-day Iran; Libya is in north Africa, west of Egypt; and Ethiopia is south of Egypt.

6. GOMER: Today the area is called Armenia. It was also known as Cappodocia, having a people called Gomer in Assyrian inscriptions.

TOGARMAH: Today's eastern Turkey (see note on Ezekiel 27:14).

7–8. PREPARE YOURSELF: This is the great time of Israel's cleansing, salvation, and spiritual life (see 39:22, 27–28; Zechariah 12:10–13:9), getting them ready for the Messiah's return and kingdom (see Zechariah 14).

8. IN THE LATTER YEARS: In the context of Israel's restoration (see Ezekiel 34–39), the invaders will make their final bid for the land.

THOSE BROUGHT BACK FROM THE SWORD: This refers to the Israelites who have been returned to their land, after the sword had killed or scattered many of their people. The Hebrew word for "brought back" means "to return" or "restore" (see Genesis 40:13; 41:13).

GATHERED: This word also frequently refers to God's final regathering of Israel (see Ezekiel 37:21; Isaiah 11:12; 43:5; Jeremiah 32:37). It has begun historically and will continue until the latter days. The full national and spiritual regathering, when all Israel is saved to enter their promised kingdom, will occur during the final millennial kingdom (see Zechariah 12–14; Romans 11:25–27).

DWELL SAFELY: This term occurs in several contexts devoted to the Israelites' blessed estate after God has brought them back to their land (see Ezekiel 28:26; 34:25, 28; 39:26; Jeremiah 32:37; Zechariah 14:11).

9. YOU WILL ASCEND, COMING LIKE A STORM: The time of this invasion is best understood as the end of the future Tribulation period of seven years. Israel will have been under a false peace in treaty with the Antichrist (see Daniel 9:27; 11:22, 24) before he turns on them in the "abomination of desolation" (Daniel 9:27; Matthew 24:15). The false peace will end in hostility that lasts to the completion of the seven years (see Zechariah 14:1–3). When this final war occurs (see Revelation 16:12–16), Christ will ultimately conquer the beast, the false prophet, and all the ungodly forces (see Revelation 19:11–21) in order to establish His millennial kingdom (see Revelation 20:1–10).

10–13. THOUGHTS WILL ARISE IN YOUR MIND: This describes the peace in Israel during the period of the Antichrist's short-lived treaty with them (see Daniel 9:27) during the first half of Daniel's seventieth week. References to "unwalled villages" refer to that period of three and one-half years when Israel is secure under the protection of the world-ruling "prince that shall come," called the Antichrist (see Daniel 9:27). After the Antichrist turns on Israel, there will be an escalation of hostility until the end of the seven-year time when this great force comes to plunder Jerusalem and the promised land (verse 12).

12. TO TAKE PLUNDER AND TO TAKE BOOTY: The Antichrist takes over the world for his own power and possession. The wealth of his empire is described in Revelation 18.

13. TARSHISH: The location of Tarshish, famous for its wealth (see Psalm 72:10; Jeremiah 10:9; Ezekiel 27:12, 25), is not known for certain. The Greek historian Herodotus identified it with Tartessus, a merchant city in southern Spain, about 2,500 miles west of Joppa.

15. RIDING ON HORSES: These could be actual horses used in war, if Tribulation judgments (seals, trumpets, vials) in Revelation 6–16 have dealt drastic blows to industries producing war vehicles and weaponry. Others see the horses and weapons here being used symbolically to represent that which would be easy to grasp in Ezekiel's day but which would be fulfilled in the future time with different war forms actually suitable to the time.

16. THAT THE NATIONS MAY KNOW ME: This phrase, used frequently in the book of Ezekiel, is part of the theme "to glorify God and show His sovereign power." God is the victor who will be "hallowed" by fire (see verse 19).

GOD'S INTERVENTION TO PROTECT ISRAEL: Ezekiel now relates how the Lord God will ultimately intervene to save Israel from the continued attacks of Gog and her allies.

17. ARE YOU HE: See notes on Ezekiel 38:2. This refers to the general references to this time and the participants (see Joel 3:9–17; Amos 5:11–12; Zephaniah 3:8). Even Daniel referred to this time at least three decades prior to Ezekiel 38 (see Daniel 2:41–44). The nature of the question presupposes that the previous generalities are now being particularized in the person of Gog.

18–23. MY FURY WILL SHOW: God's patience will be exhausted with the repeated attempts to annihilate Israel since the "abomination" by the Antichrist (see Daniel 9:27; Matthew 24:15), and He will employ a great earthquake in Israel. Panic will seize the invading soldiers (verse 21), who will turn and use their weapons against one another (see 2 Chronicles 20:22–23). God will further decimate the invading ranks by pestilence, a deluge of rain, large hailstones, and fire and brimstone. The descriptions here are identical to that of the last half of the seven-year Tribulation in Revelation 6:12–17; 11:19; 16:17–21; 19:11-21.

39:1–10. I AM AGAINST YOU: This scene of the army's ruin adds detail to Ezekiel 38:18–23, including: (1) the disarming of soldiers (verse 3), (2) their fall in death (verses 4–5), (3) the gorging of birds and beasts on the corpses (verse 4), (4) fire sent also on others besides the army (verse 6), and (5) the burning of weapons by Israelites (verses 9–10).

9. SEVEN YEARS: A vast army ("many peoples" in Ezekiel 38:15) would have much weaponry, requiring seven years to burn. Since this likely occurs at the end of the time of Tribulation, synonymous with the battle of Armageddon (see Revelation 16:16; 19:19–21), the burials (see verse 11) would extend into the millennial kingdom.

11–16. GIVE GOG A BURIAL PLACE: Israelites moving east from the Mediterranean Sea, with the sea to their backs and the Jezreel Valley before them, will bury the bodies. Further, the people in the whole land will help in the massive interment, which consumes seven months. The description fits the time after Christ's Second Advent extending into the millennial era, as those who go into His kingdom do the work (see Revelation 20:1–10).

11, 16. HAMON GOG: Literally "the multitude of Gog" (see note on Ezekiel 38:2). In verse 16, a city in the area will be named Hamonah, "multitude" (see a similar idea in Joel 3:14).

17–20. SPEAK TO EVERY . . . BIRD AND . . . BEAST: God's word summons carrion birds and carnivorous animals to consume the fallen flesh, as described in Revelation 19:21.

17–18. MY SACRIFICIAL MEAL: Since God uses the imagery of a sacrificial meal to describe this feast, the warriors who fell (verse 19) are described figuratively with words such as "rams" and other animals used in sacrifice.

21–29. I WILL SET MY GLORY: God vanquishes Israel's foes to show His glory so His enemies and Israel will all know that He is the Lord (see verses 6, 22). This is Israel's salvation spoken of in Zechariah 12:10–13:9 and Romans 11:25–27.

29. I SHALL HAVE POURED OUT MY SPIRIT: God's provision of His Spirit at the Second Advent complements the regathering (see Ezekiel 36:27; 37:14; Joel 2:28). The Gog and Magog assault in Revelation 20:7–9 at the end of the Millennium is another assault on Jerusalem patterned after certain images of the invasion here (Ezekiel 38–39), but it is a distinct event 1,000 years after the millennial kingdom begins.

UNLEASHING THE TEXT

1) What was God saying to His people through the vision of the dry bones in Ezekiel 37:1–14?

_____

_____

_____

_____

_____

_____

2) What is the meaning of the vision of the two sticks in Ezekiel 37:15–28?

_____

_____

_____

_____

_____

3) Who are the forces that will gather against Israel based on Ezekiel 38:1–17? What is the "evil plan" that they will make against God's people?

_____

_____

_____

_____

_____

4) God promises to destroy the armies that will come against Israel and free His people (see Ezekiel 39:1–16). What promise does the Lord then make to the "whole house of Israel" (see verses 21–29)?

_____

_____

_____

_____

EXPLORING THE MEANING

God brings the promise of restoration. The destruction of Jerusalem—along with the death and scattering of the people of Judah—served as a rock-bottom moment for the Jewish captives living in Babylon. Hearing the news especially of the temple's desecration made it seem as if Israel as a nation would cease to exist. The captives likely wondered if their heritage and place as God's chosen people was about to be erased from the world. However, in that moment of doubt and terror, God gave Ezekiel a vision of a valley filled with dry bones, representing the nation of Israel. In the vision, God asked a critical question: "Son of man, can these bones live?" (37:3). The rest of the vision provides an answer to that question. At God's instruction, Ezekiel prophesied to the bones, exhorting them to "hear the word of the LORD" (verse 4). Ezekiel then watched as sinew and flesh were knitted on the bones. He spoke breath into the bodies, and they were returned to life. God then gave His prophet a profound promise: "Behold, O My people, I will open your graves and cause you to come up from your graves, and bring you into the land of Israel" (verse 12). The nation of Israel would be restored.

God brings the promise of the Holy Spirit. One of the key factors involved in the restoration of Israel would be the pouring out of the Holy Spirit. In Ezekiel 36, the Lord described a when/then scenario: "I will put My Spirit within you and cause you to walk in My statutes, and you will keep My judgments and do them. Then you shall dwell in the land that I gave to your fathers; you shall be My people, and I will be your God" (verses 27–28). *When* God placed His Spirit within Israel, *then* they would dwell in the land. In Ezekiel 37, God again declared, "I will put My Spirit in you, and you shall live, and I will place you in your own land" (verse 14). In the same way that God poured out His Spirit to launch the church (see Acts 2:1–4), He will one day pour out His Spirit on Israel before fully restoring that nation during Christ's millennial kingdom.

God brings the promise of divine protection. Ezekiel 38–39 represent a new direction in the book in that they primarily point to events that are still in the future. Specifically, those chapters describe a dangerous attack from a coalition of enemies (identified as Gog and Magog) that will surround the restored nation of Israel. "You will come up against My people Israel like a cloud, to cover the land. It will be in the latter days that I will bring you against My land, so that the nations may know Me, when I am hallowed in you" (38:16). These events will occur during the final moments of the Tribulation. Under the direct influence of Satan, the Antichrist will gather a huge army that will attack Israel and ultimately surround Jerusalem. The city will be filled with those who accepted Christ during the Tribulation, including a majority of Jewish people. However, unknown to the Antichrist, this army will be gathered according to God's will and plan. In a display of fury, Christ will descend and destroy the armies arrayed against Israel, fulfilling these promises of protection for His people.

REFLECTING ON THE TEXT

5) What is the significance of God giving "breath" to the dry bones in the valley?

_____

_____

_____

_____

_____

6) How would you explain the work of the Holy Spirit in the life of a follower of Christ to someone who had never heard that concept before?

_____

_____

_____

_____

_____

7) What are some evidences of the Spirit's work in the life of a believer?

_____

_____

_____

_____

_____

_____

8) When have you seen God preserve your faith in Him through the difficulties of life? How has He protected you from the pitfalls of this world?

_____

_____

_____

_____

_____

_____

PERSONAL RESPONSE

9) Are you dependent on your own abilities and resources or on God? How can you depend on the Holy Spirit each day?

_____

_____

_____

_____

_____

10) What is your response to the Lord when you read about the restoration that He has planned?

_____

_____

_____

_____

_____

_____

10

THE NEW TEMPLE
OF THE LORD

Ezekiel 40:1–44:31

DRAWING NEAR

What was the significance of the temple in the Old Testament? What was predicted about the future of the temple?

_____

_____

_____

_____

_____

_____

_____

_____

_____

_____

_____

THE CONTEXT

As we have seen in this study, Ezekiel prophesied several times that the "remnant" of God's people—those who were scattered around the world after the invasions of Assyria and Babylon—would one day be regathered and restored to the promised land. For example, in the last lesson, we examined how God had promised,

"I will bring back the captives of Jacob, and have mercy on the whole house of Israel; and I will be jealous for My holy name—after they have borne their shame, and all their unfaithfulness in which they were unfaithful to Me, when they dwelt safely in their own land and no one made them afraid" (Ezekiel 39:25–26).

In 1948, after World War II, the United States and other countries helped reestablish Israel as a nation. This was a stunning moment, as no other nation in history had been conquered, dissolved, settled, and resettled over a period of more than 1,000 years—and then restored to its ancient heritage. This reestablishment demonstrates the Lord's preservation of His people against all odds and is a preview of the future regathering that Ezekiel prophesizes. God has promised this coming restoration to the land, the spiritual restoration of the Jewish people, and the glorious restoration of the temple in Jerusalem. These promises were given to Ezekiel through a powerful vision in which he witnessed an angel measure the dimensions of that future temple—a prophetic promise that will ultimately be fulfilled during the Millennium.

Ezekiel 40–48 describes this millennial reign of Christ, giving more details about the 1,000-year kingdom than all other Old Testament prophecies combined. It is the "Holy of Holies" among millennial forecasts. As with the previous chapters in Ezekiel, this concluding portion will be approached in a literal and historical manner, which best serves the interpreter in all Scripture. In many ways, these chapters are the most important in the book. They form the crowning reality—the climax of Ezekiel's prophecy and Israel's restoration.

KEYS TO THE TEXT

Read Ezekiel 40:1–44:31, noting the key words and phrases indicated below.

NEW CITY AND TEMPLE: In another vision, Ezekiel is taken to a high mountain in Israel and shown a new holy city and temple.

40:1. THE TWENTY-FIFTH YEAR: 573 BC, in the first month of the ecclesiastical year, Nisan. The tenth day was the start of preparations for Passover.

2. IN THE VISIONS OF GOD HE TOOK ME: In Ezekiel 40–48, the prophet narrates another vision that he received, just as before in Ezekiel 1:1–3:27; 8–11; 37:1–14. The characterization of the prophecy as a vision in no way detracts from its literal reality any more than Ezekiel's visions of Jerusalem's sins, idolatry, and destruction did in previous chapters.

INTO THE LAND OF ISRAEL: The vision pertains to Israel, as in Ezekiel 1–24; 33; 34–39.

A VERY HIGH MOUNTAIN: The mountain is not named; however, it is most likely Mount Zion (see Ezekiel 17:22; 20:40; Isaiah 2:2; Micah 4:1), lifted up from its surroundings by a great earthquake (see Zechariah 14:4–5, 10).

LIKE THE STRUCTURE . . . A CITY: God will be explaining details related to Israel's spiritual future (see verses 2, 4), so this must refer to the temple in particular and Jerusalem in general. This new and glorious temple will stand in contrast to the desecration and destruction of Solomon's temple (see Ezekiel 8–11).

3. A MAN: An angel conducted a tour of all the details seen by the prophet, appearing in the form of a man (see Genesis 18; Ezekiel 9) and appearing like bright and gleaming bronze. He could be understood as the Angel of the Lord, since he is later called "LORD" (44:2, 5). His "line of flax" was for larger measurements, while his "rod" was for shorter ones (see Revelation 11:1; 21:5). In each case, God measured what belonged to Him.

4. DECLARE . . . EVERYTHING YOU SEE: Chapters 1–24 in Ezekiel refers to Israel's historical removal from her land, chapters 25–32 to historical judgments against other nations, and chapter 33 to a historical call to repentance and the fall of Jerusalem. So, the most natural way to interpret chapters 34–39 is Israel's literal future return to the same land as a reversal of the historical dispersion. Ezekiel 38 and 39 describe a future historical invasion of Israel and its aftermath during the time just before the Messiah's return. Chapters 40–48 thus continue this historical, prophetic pattern, describing the millennial conditions after the Messiah comes and destroys the ungodly (see Revelation 19:11ff.), under which Israel will live and worship. Believing Gentiles will also be in the kingdom as sheep of the Great Shepherd (see Matthew 25:31–46), while all unbelievers are destroyed. Ezekiel is to write down all the details.

5. A WALL ALL AROUND: This outer wall is later described as a separation of the holy areas (see Ezekiel 42:20).

THE TEMPLE: Compare the details of this temple with the details of Solomon's temple in 1 Kings 6–7. This could not refer to the heavenly temple, since Ezekiel was taken to Israel to see it (see verse 2). It could not be Zerubbabel's temple, since the glory of God was not present at that time. It could not be the eternal temple, since the Lord and the Lamb are its temple (see Revelation 21:22). Therefore, it must be the earthly, millennial temple built with all of the exquisite details that are yet to be outlined.

MEASURING ROD SIX CUBITS LONG . . . A HANDBREADTH: The rod extended six royal (long) cubits of twenty-one inches for a total of ten and one-half feet, with each cubit being made up of a standard width of eighteen inches and a handbreadth of three inches.

6–7. THE GATEWAY . . . EAST: The buildings of the east gate are first because this will be in the direct line of approach to the temple. Each opening was ten and one-half feet across. Chambers (rooms) in the wall are ten and one-half feet by ten and one-half feet. Precise measurements like these describe a literal temple, not a symbolic one.

8–16. MEASURED THE VESTIBULE: The chambers described in this section are accommodations for the ministering priests and temple officers who care for the temple.

16. BEVELED WINDOW FRAMES: Since they had no glass, these are lattices (see Ezekiel 41:16–26).

AND ON EACH GATEPOST WERE PALM TREES: These depict God's desire for fruit in Israel. Palms are symbols of beauty, salvation, and triumph (see Zechariah 14:16ff.; Revelation 7:9). Palms are on the inner court's gateposts as well (see verse 31).

17–37. THE OUTER COURT: This court is farthest out from the temple proper and enclosed by the outer walls. What follows is a further blueprint for the temple area, with more precise measurements. The numbers 5, 25, 50, and 100 are frequently used. The sanctuary formed a square of some 500 cubits.

38–47: THERE WAS A CHAMBER: This section describes "chambers" for the priests, raising the question of sacrifices in the millennial kingdom. Such sacrifices will exist, as verses 39–43 indicate, but will be no more efficacious here than they were in Old Testament times. No sacrifices before or after Christ could save—they could only point to Him as the one true Lamb who takes away sin. Just as the Lord's Supper is a memorial that looks back to Calvary but in no way diminishes the cross, so the Jews who have received Jesus as their Messiah and are in His kingdom will have a memorial of sacrifices that point to Him. They will have missed the memorial of the Lord's Supper but will have their own memorial sacrifices for 1,000 years.

39. BURNT OFFERING . . . SIN OFFERING . . . TRESPASS OFFERING: For their Old Testament background, see (1) Leviticus 1:1–17; 6:8–13; (2) Leviticus 4:1–35; 6:24–30; and (3) Leviticus 5:1–6:7; 7:1–10, respectively. (See also Ezekiel 43:18–27; 45:13–25; 46:1–15, 19–24.)

41. TABLES ON WHICH THEY SLAUGHTERED: Four tables are on either side of the inner court's north gate, used for commemorating the death of Christ by offering burnt, sin, and trespass offerings.

44. SINGERS: Provision is made for the praises of the redeemed in music.

46. SONS OF ZADOK: Proper names such as "Zadok" tie the vision to historical reality, calling for literal interpretation. This Levitical family descended from Levi, Aaron, Eleazar, and Phinehas (see 1 Chronicles 6:3–8). In accord with God's covenant with Phinehas (see Numbers 25:10–13), and because of Eli's unfaithfulness (see 1 Samuel 1; 2) and Zadok's faithfulness to David and Solomon (see 1 Kings 1:32–40), Zadok's sons serve as priests in the millennial temple. Other references to sons of Zadok are found in Ezekiel 43:19; 44:15; 48:11.

47. MEASURED THE COURT: The court around the square temple was also a square (see 41:1).

ALTAR: This is the bronze altar where offerings are made (see 43:13–27).

48–49. VESTIBULE: This refers to the temple porch and is similar to that of Solomon's temple.

TEMPLE AREA: Ezekiel's descriptions continue for the temple proper, its sanctuary or holy place, and side chambers for priests' quarters.

41:1. INTO THE SANCTUARY: This chapter in Ezekiel can again be studied in the light of 1 Kings 6–7 to note differences from Solomon's temple.

4. THE MOST HOLY PLACE: The Holy of Holies, which the high priest entered annually on the Day of Atonement (see Leviticus 16). These dimensions are identical to Solomon's temple (see 1 Kings 6:20) and twice those of the tabernacle in the wilderness.

5–11. THE WALL OF THE TEMPLE: This section describes the wall and the side chambers.

12. BUILDING . . . AT ITS WESTERN END: Beyond the western end of the temple proper was a distinct building with space that served the temple, possibly housing supplies.

13. MEASURED THE TEMPLE: See Ezekiel 40:47. It was about 175 feet square.

15. ITS GALLERIES: These were terraced buildings with decorations (see verses 18–20).

18. CHERUBIM AND PALM TREES: Figures of angels (see Ezekiel 1; 10) with palms between them (possibly to depict life and fruitfulness of God's servants) were on the walls of the temple proper and on the doors (see verse 25). Each cherub (unlike that of Ezekiel 1; 10, which had four faces) had the face of a man and of a lion, possibly to represent the humanity and kingship of the Messiah.

22. THE ALTAR: This is the altar of incense (see Exodus 30:1–3; 1 Kings 7:48).

42:3–14. GALLERY AGAINST GALLERY: Priestly rooms are now described (see verses 3–12), situated along the south, north, and west walls of the sanctuary and Most Holy Place, in three stories. Priests eat the holy offerings (see Leviticus 2:3, 10; 6:9–11; 10:12) and dress there (see verses 13–14).

15–20. OUT THROUGH THE GATEWAY: The angel measured the height and thickness of the outside wall (see Ezekiel 40:5), then the outer court (see 40:6–27), then the inner court with the chambers (see 40:28–42:14), and finally, the extent of all the temple buildings outside. Measurements of the outer wall, 500 rods each way, were approximately one mile on each of the four sides. Much too large for Mount Moriah, this scheme will require changes in the topography of Jerusalem, as Zechariah predicted (see Zechariah 14:9–11).

43:2. THE GLORY OF THE GOD OF ISRAEL: In earlier chapters of Ezekiel's prophecy, emphasis was given to the departure of God's glory from the temple (see chapters 8–11). Thus, the Lord abandoned His people to destruction and dispersion. Here, in the millennial temple, the glory of God returns to dwell. His glory will be manifest in fullness in the future kingdom, after the Lord's Second Advent, which is also to be glorious (see Matthew 16:27; 25:31). Verses 1–12 describe God's glorious entrance into the sanctuary.

CAME FROM . . . THE EAST: The glory had been in the tabernacle (see Exodus 40:34, 35) and the temple (see 1 Kings 8:10–11), though not in Zerubbabel's temple. Here, the Lord returns to be Israel's king. The glory departed to the east from Israel (see Ezekiel 11:23) when God judged the people, so the glory returns from the east when He has regathered them and is restoring their worship.

3. LIKE THE . . . VISION: This vision appearance of God to Ezekiel is glorious, just as the vision in chapters 8–11, which pictures His coming, by angels, to judge Jerusalem (see Ezekiel 9:3–11; 10:4–7).

LIKE THE VISION . . . BY THE RIVER CHEBAR: God's appearance is also glorious as in the vision of Ezekiel 1:3–28.

I FELL ON MY FACE: Just as in the other visions of God's glory (see 1:28; 9:8).

5. THE GLORY . . . FILLED THE TEMPLE: The future kingdom glory of God will fill His temple (see Zechariah 2:5), just as He filled Moses' tabernacle (see Exodus 40:34) and later Solomon's temple (see 1 Kings 8:11; Psalm 29:9).

7. THIS IS THE PLACE OF MY THRONE: The King of glory (see Psalm 24:7–10) claims the millennial temple as His place to dwell (see 1 Chronicles 29:23; Zechariah 6:13). There will be human, unresurrected people in the kingdom, who entered when Christ returned and destroyed all the wicked. They will worship at this actual temple.

8–9. HARLOTRY . . . CARCASSES OF THEIR KINGS: The future temple will be most holy, protected from (1) harlotry such as that in which the Israelites had engaged (see 2 Kings 23:7), and (2) defiling tombs of kings that Israel had allowed in the sacred temple area (see Ezekiel 21:18).

10–12. DESCRIBE THE TEMPLE TO THE HOUSE OF ISRAEL: Here is the key to the entire vision of Ezekiel 40–48. These glorious future plans show how much Israel had forfeited by their sins. Every detail should produce repentance in Ezekiel's hearers and readers.

TRUE WORSHIP: Ezekiel, having now described the holy city and temple in detail, turns to describing the true worship of God that will take place there.

13–27. THE ALTAR: The measurements of the altar of burnt offering are given in verses 13–17, and then the offerings are described in verses 18–27. These offerings are not efficacious, nor were the Old Testament sacrifices, but they were all symbolic of death for sin. They do not take away sin (see Hebrews 10:4). They were prospective; these will be retrospective.

19. A YOUNG BULL FOR A SIN OFFERING: Exact offerings are given in language just as definitive as the literal descriptions in Moses' day. These offerings are of a memorial nature; again, they are not efficacious any more than the Old Testament sacrifices were. Just as the Old Testament sacrifices pointed forward to Christ's death, so these are tangible expressions, not competing with but pointing back to, the value of Christ's completely effective sacrifice, once for all (see Hebrews 9:28; 10:10). In the Old Testament, God endorsed offerings as tokens of forgiving and cleansing worshipers on the basis and credit of the great Lamb they pointed forward to, who alone could take away sins (see John 1:29). The tangible expressions of worship, which the Israelites for so long failed to offer validly (see Isaiah 1:11–15), will at last be offered acceptably, and with full understanding about the Lamb of God to whom they point.

SEED OF ZADOK: See notes on Ezekiel 40:46.

24. SALT: See Leviticus 2:13.

BURNT OFFERING: Just as the sin offering is a part of future millennial worship (see verse 19), so there are other offerings as well (see Leviticus 1–7). One of these is the burnt offering, which denotes the person's full consecration to God. Another is the peace offering, in which the person expresses gratitude for peace with God in covenant bonds (see verse 27).

25. WITHOUT BLEMISH: This is commemorative of Jesus Christ's unblemished perfection.

44:1–2. THE OUTER GATE . . . WAS SHUT: The Lord has now returned from the direction in which He departed (see Ezekiel 10:18–19). The gate is kept closed in honor of the Lord's glory having returned through it for the millennial worship and to indicate that the Lord will not depart from it again, as in Ezekiel 8–11 (see also 43:1–5). This eastern gate of the temple should not be confused with the modern sealed eastern gate of the city (see 45:6–8).

3. THE PRINCE . . . MAY SIT IN IT: The designation "prince" is used at least fourteen times in Ezekiel 44–47. This "prince" is not the Lord Jesus Christ but someone distinct from Him. This is seen in the fact that he will "eat bread before the LORD," he has sins for which he offers sacrifice (see 45:22), and he fathers sons (see 46:16–18). He cannot enter by the east gate that the Lord used, but he is allowed to come in and go out by the gate's vestibule and eat bread by the gateway. He cannot perform priestly duties (see 45:19) as the Messiah will (see Psalm 110:4; Zechariah 6:12–13), and he must worship the Lord (see Ezekiel 46:2). Most likely, the prince is neither a priest nor the king but is one who administrates the kingdom, representing the King (the Lord Jesus Christ) on one hand, and also the princes (see 14:8–9) who individually lead the twelve tribes. Possibly, he will be a descendant of David.

5–9. MARK WELL WHO MAY ENTER: Since the Lord's glory fills the temple, it is sanctified (see verse 4), and God is particular about what kind of people worship there. Sins of the past, as in Ezekiel 8–11, must not be repeated and, if they are, will exclude their perpetrators from the temple. Only the circumcised in heart may enter (see Deuteronomy 30:6; Jeremiah 4:4; Romans 2:25–29), whether of Israel or another nation (verses 7, 9). Many other peoples than Jews will go into the kingdom in unresurrected bodies, because they have believed in Jesus Christ and were ready for His coming. They will escape His deadly judgment and populate and reproduce in the 1,000-year kingdom. Such circumcision pertains to a heart that is sincere about removing sin and being devoted to the

Lord (see Jeremiah 29:13). In the Millennium, a Jew with an uncircumcised heart will be considered a foreigner (verse 9). "Uncircumcised in flesh" refers to sinners and "foreigner" identifies rejecters of the true God.

10–15. LEVITES . . . SHALL BEAR THEIR INIQUITY: God makes distinctions. Levites in the line of those who were unfaithful before the judgment can minister in temple services but cannot make offerings or enter the Most Holy Place (verses 11–14). Only Zadok's line can fulfill those ministries (verses 15–16). The reason for this is the value that God attaches to the faithfulness of Zadok in the past (see 1 Samuel 2:35; 2 Samuel 15:24ff.; 1 Kings 1:32–40; 2:26–35; see also note on Ezekiel 40:46).

16. MY TABLE: This is the altar of burnt offering (see 40:46; 41:22).

17–27. IT SHALL BE: Various standards govern priestly service, such as moderation (verse 20) and sobriety (verse 21). The priests will model holy behavior as they teach the people to live their lives set apart to God (verses 23–24). Minutiae about dress (such as forbidding the uncleanness of sweat resulting from wearing wool), marriage (see Leviticus 21:14), contact with dead bodies, and the like point more naturally to a literal fulfillment than to a generalized blurring of details in a symbolical interpretation.

28–31. I AM THEIR POSSESSION: As the priests had no possession in the land when it was originally apportioned, so in the future God will be their portion.

UNLEASHING THE TEXT

1) How does Ezekiel describe the "man" who appeared to him in his vision (see Ezekiel 40:3)? What instructions did this man then give to Ezekiel (see verse 4)?

_____

_____

_____

_____

2) Ezekiel provides descriptions and measurements of the millennial temple in 40:5–43:12. Which features stand out the most? Why are they significant?

_____

_____

_____

_____

3) Ezekiel describes worship in the new temple in 43:18–27. How should we understand the provisions for animal sacrifice as part of this worship?

_____

_____

_____

_____

4) What do you learn about God from the regulations given in Ezekiel 44:10–31?

_____

_____

_____

_____

EXPLORING THE MEANING

There will be a literal temple in the Millennium. There is disagreement among scholars regarding the identity of the temple described in Ezekiel's vision. Some believe the vision highlighted Solomon's temple. Others believe it to be Zerubbabel's temple, which was rebuilt after the Jewish exiles returned to the promised land. Still others believe it to be a vision of the eternal state described in Revelation 21–22. However, the text itself rules out these possibilities. We know this is not Solomon's temple because that structure had been destroyed by Nebuchadnezzar's armies many years before, and the primary thrust of Ezekiel's visions in this section of the book are focused forward on the future restoration of Israel. We know this cannot be Zerubbabel's temple because the glory of the Lord never entered that place. And we know this cannot describe our eternal state because John specifically states, "But I saw no temple in it, for the Lord God Almighty and the Lamb are its temple" (Revelation 21:22). Therefore, we can say with certainty that Ezekiel's vision points forward to a literal, physical temple that will be present during the thousand-year millennial reign of Christ.

The relationship between God and His people will be restored. In a previous lesson, we examined a critical moment in Ezekiel's prophecy in which he described the glory of the LORD departing from the temple in Jerusalem (see Ezekiel 8–11). God had removed His glory from the temple because of His people's continual worship of false gods. However, in describing this future temple, Ezekiel makes several references to the *renewed* presence of God's glory that will be there: "And behold, the glory of the God of Israel came from the way of the east. His voice was like the sound of many waters; and the earth shone with His glory" (43:2). There is a clear effort in Ezekiel's vision to show the restoration of what God's people had lost because of their sin—which included not only the temple but also the presence of God in their midst. During the Millennium, the relationship between God and the Jewish people will be restored.

God desires all His people to return to Him. It is worth asking why Ezekiel received this extended vision of the temple at this specific moment in his people's history. We know from the text that Ezekiel's vision took place "in the fourteenth year after the city was captured" (40:1). Thus, one reason for the timing of the vision was to offer hope to the captives—to reveal a future time in which everything they had lost would be restored and even improved. However, God identified a second reason: "Son of man, describe the temple to the house of Israel, that they may be ashamed of their iniquities; and let them measure the pattern. And if they are ashamed of all that they have done, make known to them the design of the temple and its arrangement, its exits and its entrances, its entire design and all its ordinances, all its forms and all its laws" (43:10–11). God wanted His people to acknowledge that they had rebelled against Him. He then wanted them to repent of their sins and fully return to Him.

REFLECTING ON THE TEXT

5) What do the detailed dimensions of the temple in this passage reveal about it? Why does this suggest that it refers to a physical temple?

_____

_____

_____

_____

_____

6) How should the reality of the future Millennium impact your actions today?

_____

_____

_____

_____

7) What are some ways you can tell others of God's glory today?

_____

_____

_____

_____

_____

8) Jesus said one of the roles of the Holy Spirit is to "convict the world of sin" (John 16:8). What purpose does conviction serve? What benefits does it produce?

_____

_____

_____

_____

_____

PERSONAL RESPONSE

9) The restoration of Israel is a major theme in this portion of Ezekiel's prophecy. What does God's relationship with Israel teach you about His character and His relationship to you?

_____

_____

_____

_____

_____

10) What does this section of Ezekiel say about God's willingness to forgive you of your sins? How do you receive that forgiveness from Him?

_____

_____

_____

_____

_____

11

THE HOLY DISTRICT AND LAND REDISTRIBUTION

Ezekiel 45:1–48:35

DRAWING NEAR

In what ways does your society fall short of what God calls it to be? How does God promise to correct those issues in His coming kingdom?

_____

_____

_____

_____

_____

_____

_____

_____

_____

_____

_____

_____

THE CONTEXT

In the previous lesson, we discussed how the final eight chapters in the book of Ezekiel provide explicit details about the Millennium—the 1,000-year period when Jesus will reign on earth. Ezekiel 40–43 features extensive details about the new temple that will be present during this time. The prophet related how he was taken "into the land of Israel" and set "on a very high mountain" where he could see this new city of God and its temple (Ezekiel 40:2). An angel then measured the dimensions of that temple and each of its primary structures.

After Ezekiel recorded each of the dimensions given to him by the angel, "the glory of the God of Israel came from the way of the east" (43:2). The Lord then revealed the purpose of Ezekiel recording all these measurements: "Son of man, describe the temple to the house of Israel, that they may be ashamed of their iniquities; and let them measure the pattern" (verse 10). These glorious future plans revealed to the people of Israel just how much they had forfeited because of their sins. Every detail was to produce repentance in their hearts.

In this lesson, we will explore how the remaining chapters of Ezekiel's prophetic record describe the new holy district that will be created and the role of the "prince" or administrator of that district. We will examine the new system of feasts that will be instituted (chapters 45–46). We will then discuss the redistribution of the promised land among God's people (chapters 47–48). In the end, we will find that while the primary audience for Ezekiel's prophecies and visions was the Jewish people, they still have relevance for Christians today.

KEYS TO THE TEXT

Read Ezekiel 45:1–48:35, noting the key words and phrases indicated below.

> THE HOLY DISTRICT: *Ezekiel next describes a sacred portion of land that will be set apart in the millennial kingdom, including territory for an administrator.*

45:1–5. SET APART A DISTRICT FOR THE LORD: This sacred land, which is set apart at the heart (center) of Palestine, is separate from the allotments designated for various tribes—seven to the north and five to the south (see Ezekiel 48). Although the whole earth is the Lord's (see Psalm 24:1), this area is meaningful to Him in a special sense, providing for special purposes that are defined in Ezekiel 45:2–8. This holy rectangle (8.5 miles by 3.3 miles) corresponds to Ezekiel 48:8–22, which describes this portion of land as between Judah to the north and Benjamin to the south, extending from the Mediterranean Sea east to the border. It is the area for the priestly homes (verse 4) particularly, but is also for the benefit of all worshipers.

2. A . . . PLOT FOR THE SANCTUARY: At the heart of the special allotment is the temple area (see 48:10). This area serves all the Israelite tribes and also is the worship center for those in the whole world who visit (see Isaiah 4:2–3; Zechariah 14:16–19). It is one mile square (see Ezekiel 42:15–20). As a center for those in Palestine and for the world, the area is appropriately larger than past temples that served Israel.

5. TO THE LEVITES: Distinct from the land devoted to the temple and priestly homes is another portion for Levites, who assist in temple service. This portion is also about 8.5 miles by 3.3 miles and lies north of the temple/priest allotment. (See 48:13–14 for more details.)

6. PROPERTY OF THE CITY: On the south of the central sanctuary plot is the city of Jerusalem with an area of about 8.5 miles by 1.65 miles. (See 48:15–20 for more details.)

7. THE PRINCE SHALL HAVE A SECTION: See note on Ezekiel 44:3. This administrator of the kingdom under Christ will have his territory in two parts: one to the west, and the other to the east of the temple, priest, and city portions of verses 1–6. (See 48:21–22 for more details.)

8. MY PRINCES SHALL NO MORE OPPRESS: God pledges a kingdom era free from civil leaders who selfishly take advantage of the people (see Ezekiel 22:27; Numbers 36:7–9; 1 Kings 21; Isaiah 5:8; Hosea 5:10; Micah 2:1–2). The princes most likely are the leaders of each tribe. No one will be deprived of his possession under the Messiah's rule.

9–12. YOU SHALL HAVE HONEST SCALES: The leaders of the land are urged to be thoroughly honest in their commercial dealings. This warning shows that there will be sin in the Millennium. The believing Jews who entered the 1,000-year reign of Christ on earth and inherited the promised kingdom will be fully human and, therefore, capable of such sins. There also will be children who do not necessarily believe, as the final rebellion against King Messiah and His temple proves (see Revelation 20:7–9).

10. SCALES: Relates to selling by weight.

EPHAH: Relates to selling by dry volume.

BATH: Relates to selling by liquid volume.

11. EPHAH . . . BATH . . . ONE-TENTH OF A HOMER: The homer, in liquid volume, is about sixty gallons; in dry volume, it is about seven and one-half of a bushel. Thus, the ephah will be set at about three-fourths of a bushel, and the bath will be set at about six gallons.

12. SHEKEL . . . GERAHS: By weight, the shekel is about 0.4 ounce made up of twenty gerahs (.02 ounce/each). Sixty shekels (20 + 25 + 15) equal a mina, or about twenty-four ounces (one and one-half pounds).

13–15. THE OFFERING WHICH YOU SHALL OFFER: Here are the offerings for Israel's prince (verse 16). Because of what the people will give him, he will provide for public sacrifices (verse 17). The people will give 1/60th of their grain (verse 13) and 1 percent of their oil (verse 14). They will give one lamb for every 200 in the flock or one-half of 1 percent (verse 15).

16–17. PRINCE: See note on Ezekiel 44:3.

18–19. THUS SAYS THE LORD: The annual feasts for the nations are outlined. The millennial feasts include three of the six Levitical feasts: (1) Passover, (2) Unleavened Bread, and (3) Tabernacles. Three Levitical feasts are not celebrated: (1) Pentecost, (2) Trumpets, and (3) Atonement. Most likely, they are excluded because what they had looked forward to prophetically has now been fulfilled and so no longer serves any significant remembrance purpose such as the Passover, Unleavened Bread, and Tabernacles will continue to provide.

18–20. ATONEMENT: The Day of Atonement is never mentioned in this section, but God institutes a never-before-celebrated festival to start the "new year" with an emphasis on holiness in the temple. The first month, Abib, would be in March/April. The feast appears to last seven days (verse 20). This again indicates that there will be sin in the kingdom, committed by those who entered alive and by their offspring.

21–24. PASSOVER . . . UNLEAVENED BREAD: The feasts of Passover and Unleavened Bread are combined as in the New Testament and focus on remembering God's deliverance of the nation from Egypt and Christ's death providing deliverance from sin. They continue on into the Millennium as a week-long feast of remembrance, which will serve much the same purpose then as the bread and cup do now (see Exodus 12–15 for details). The three annual pilgrimage feasts with required attendance under Mosaic legislation were: (1) Unleavened Bread, (2) Pentecost, and (3) Tabernacles (see Exodus 23:14–17; Numbers 28:16–29:40; Deuteronomy 16:1–17). These have been modified with the three feasts in Ezekiel 45:18–25. Pentecost is replaced by the new feast of verses 18–20. There are also portion differences from the Mosaic law (see Numbers 28:19–21), plus the millennial offerings are richer and more abundant in general.

22–23. THE PRINCE: See the note on Ezekiel 44:3. Here, the prince sacrifices for his own sin.

24. HIN: About one gallon.

25. THE SEVENTH MONTH: The Feast of Tabernacles continues on into the Millennium, as confirmed by Zechariah 14:16–21. This would be a remembrance of God's sustaining provision in the wilderness. The seventh month, Tishri, would be in September/October, and this feast will last for one week, as do the previous two. The prince ("he," verse 25) once again offers sacrifice.

MANNER OF WORSHIP: Ezekiel further discusses offerings and deals with the Sabbath and New Moon, appointed feast days, voluntary offerings, and daily sacrifices.

46: 1. THE GATEWAY . . . SHALL BE SHUT: Shutting the gate for six days seems to serve the purpose of giving special distinction to the Sabbath and New Moon, when it is open and in use. Israel largely failed and was judged in ancient times in regard to these days (see Jeremiah 17:22–27; 2 Chronicles 36:21). The Sabbath will be reinstated for a restored and regenerated Israel. Note here that modern-day sabbatarians often fail to realize that the Sabbath consisted of far more than just rest from labor and included specific sacrifices. It is inconsistent to take one part of the Sabbath observance and discard the others. (See Numbers 28:1–15 for a summary of all the former Mosaic details.)

2. THE PRINCE: See note on Ezekiel 44:3. He appears five times here (verses 2, 4, 8, 10, 12) in regard to sacrifices. He is to be an example of spiritual integrity to the people (see verse 10).

6–7. NEW MOON: Israel's calendar was lunar, so the feasts were reckoned according to the phases of the moon.

8. WHEN THE PRINCE ENTERS: The prince does not normally use the eastern gate itself, which is for the Lord (see 44:2). Rather, he enters and exits by the gate's vestibule. However, his use of the gate is permitted for freewill offerings.

9. THE PEOPLE: The people's entering and exiting for temple worship are to be done in an orderly flow to prevent congestion, since all will be present (see Deuteronomy 16:16).

10–12. THE PRINCE . . . WHEN THEY GO IN, HE SHALL GO IN: The prince sets the example of worship for the people.

13–15. YOU SHALL DAILY MAKE A BURNT OFFERING: The testimony of the Old Testament is that to remove the continual burnt offering meant an abolition of public worship (see Daniel 8:11–13; 11:31; 12:11).

16–17. IF THE PRINCE GIVES A GIFT: This explains inheritance laws governing the prince. A gift to one of his sons is permanent (verse 16), but a gift to a servant lasts only to the year of Jubilee, the fiftieth year (see Leviticus 25:10–13), and then it returns to him (verse 17).

17. THE YEAR OF LIBERTY: The year of Jubilee.

18. THE PRINCE SHALL NOT TAKE ANY . . . INHERITANCE: As in Ezekiel 45:8–9, the prince is not to confiscate others' property to enlarge his own holdings, as often occurred in Israel's history when rulers became rich by making others poor (see 1 Kings 21).

19–24. CHAMBERS: The priests' kitchen chambers, possibly close to the inner east gate, are convenient for managing their parts of the offerings and cooking sacrificial meals for worshipers. The "ministers of the temple" (verse 24) are not the priests but temple servants.

> *POSITION OF THE RIVER: This section reveals that in the millennial kingdom, amazing physical and geographical changes will occur on the earth, especially in the land of Israel. Ezekiel's words here deal mainly with changes in the water.*

47:1. BACK TO THE DOOR OF THE TEMPLE: This section reinforces the constant emphasis of the prophets that in the final kingdom, amazing physical and geographical changes will occur on the earth, especially in the land of Israel. This chapter deals mainly with changes in the water.

1–2. WATER, FLOWING . . . EAST: A stream of water flows up from underneath the temple (see Joel 3:18), going east to the Jordan River, and then curving south through the Dead Sea area (see verses 7–8). Zechariah 14:8 refers to this stream as flowing from Jerusalem to the west (Mediterranean Sea) as well as to the east (Dead Sea). Its origin coincides with Christ's Second Advent arrival on the Mount of Olives (see Zechariah 14:4; Acts 1:11), which will trigger a massive earthquake, thus creating a vast east-west valley running through Jerusalem and allowing for the water flow.

3–5. HE MEASURED: The escorting angel in the vision, wanting to reveal the size of the river, took Ezekiel to four different distances from the temple where the stream was found to be at increasing depths, until it was over his head. (See Isaiah 35:1–7, where the prophet says the "desert will blossom like a rose.")

7. VERY MANY TREES: Lush growth from the river.

8. WATERS ARE HEALED: The flow of the water east and then south will run into the Dead Sea, where it will literally refresh the salty water (more than six times as salty as the sea) that formerly could not support life because of its high mineral content. The Dead Sea is transformed into a "living sea" of fresh water.

9. MULTITUDE OF FISH: These fish are believed to be the same kinds as in the Mediterranean Sea (see verse 10), probably referring to volume rather than species, since the river and the Dead Sea are now fresh water.

10. EN GEDI: An oasis on the western shore of the Dead Sea, about halfway along its length near Masada, where there is a freshwater spring and lush vineyards (see Song of Solomon 1:14) that stand in stark contrast to the surrounding wilderness. The limestone that dominates this region is permeated with caves, which provided good hiding places for David in his day (see 1 Samuel 23:29).

EN EGLAIM: Possibly this refers to Ein-Feska near Qumran at the northwestern extremity of the sea. Some argue for a site on the east bank, so that fishermen on both sides are in view.

11. SWAMPS AND MARSHES . . . GIVEN OVER TO SALT: This could supply salt for the temple offerings (see Ezekiel 43:24) as well as for food.

12. ALL KINDS OF TREES: See verse 7. The scene describes the blessing of returning to Eden-like abundance (Genesis 2:8–9, 16).

LEAVES WILL NOT WITHER . . . FRUIT SHALL NOT FAIL: See verse 7. The fruit is for food and the leaves serve a medicinal purpose, probably both in preventative and corrective senses. The fruit is perpetual, kept so by a continual and lavish supply of spring water from the temple.

> PORTIONS FOR THE TRIBES: The picture Ezekiel presents is an enlarged Canaan for all to inhabit. The boundaries are substantially larger than those given to Moses (see Numbers 24:1–15).

13. BORDERS: Palestine, as promised in God's covenant with Abraham (see Genesis 12:7), has specific geographical limits, within which Israel will finally occupy tribal areas that differ from in Joshua's day (see Joshua 13–22).

JOSEPH SHALL HAVE TWO PORTIONS: This is in keeping with the promise of Jacob to Joseph (see Genesis 48:5–6, 22; 49:22–26).

15–20. THIS SHALL BE THE BORDER: The borders of the millennial promised land are here described: (1) to the north (verses 15–17), (2) to the east (verse 18), (3) to the south (verse 19), and (4) to the west (verse 20).

22. BEAR CHILDREN: Children will be born throughout the 1,000-year rule of Christ. Not all will believe and be saved, as evidenced by the final rebellion (see Revelation 20:8–9).

23. STRANGER: This provision is in keeping with Leviticus 19:34.

48:1–7, 23–29. THE TRIBES: The land pledged to each tribe within the total area described in Ezekiel 47:13–23 fulfills God's promises to actually restore Israel's people from around the world to the promised land just as they were actually scattered from it (see 28:25–26; 34–37; 39:21–29; Jeremiah 31:33). Dan is first mentioned. Though omitted from the 144,000 in Revelation 7, probably because of severe idolatry, Dan is restored in grace.

8–22. THE DISTRICT: Already described in Ezekiel 45:1–8, this unique area includes land allotment for the sentry and Zadokian priests (verses 8–12), the Levites (verses 13–14), the city (verses 15–20), and the prince (verses 21–22).

30–35. THESE ARE THE EXITS: Twelve city gates, three in each cardinal direction, bear the names of Israel's tribes, one on each gate.

30. FOUR THOUSAND FIVE HUNDRED CUBITS: All four sides, when added together, equal 18,000 cubits (see verse 16), which is nearly a six-mile perimeter. Josephus, a Jewish historian, reported in the first century AD that Jerusalem was approximately four miles in perimeter.

35. THE NAME: The city is called YHWH Shammah, "THE LORD IS THERE." The departed glory of God (Ezekiel 8–11) has returned (44:1–2), and His dwelling, the temple, is in the very center of the district given over to the Lord. With this final note, all the unconditional promises that God had made to Israel in the Abrahamic covenant, the priestly covenant, the Davidic covenant, and the New Covenant have been fulfilled. So, this final verse provides the consummation of Israel's history—the returned presence of God!

UNLEASHING THE TEXT

1) Did it surprise you to learn there will be a holy district in the millennial kingdom and a "prince" who will administrate it? Who is the prince, and what is his role?

_____

_____

_____

_____

_____

2) Why do you think Ezekiel went into such detail in his description of the millennial temple, city, and land? How does this point to the fact that this will be a *literal* place?

_____

_____

_____

_____

_____

_____

3) Which of the feasts will be celebrated during the millennial kingdom (see Ezekiel 45:18–25)? Why will the feasts of Pentecost, Trumpets, and Atonement no longer be celebrated?

_____

_____

_____

_____

_____

4) Ezekiel 48, the final chapter, deals with the division of the land during the Millennium. Why would that have especially interested Ezekiel's readers?

_____

_____

_____

_____

_____

EXPLORING THE MEANING

God will be present in the millennial kingdom. In describing the land of the millennial kingdom, Ezekiel mentions a special district that will be set apart at the center of Israel: "When you divide the land by lot into inheritance, you shall set apart a district for the LORD, a holy section of the land; its length shall be twenty-five thousand cubits, and the width ten thousand" (45:1). In ancient Israel, God's temple was set aside and hallowed as the place in which God's name, or presence, dwelt among His people. During the Millennium, this holy district will measure 8.5 miles by 3.3 miles—a huge area representing a "Holy of Holies" within the earth as a whole. This district will include the millennial temple itself, housing for the priests, housing for the prince, and more. It will represent a vast increase in God's physical and tangible presence in our world. Of course, that presence will be fully realized in the person of Jesus Christ, who will reign over all the earth from Jerusalem, seated on the throne of King David (see 2 Samuel 7). As Ezekiel summed it up, "The name of the city from that day shall be: THE LORD IS THERE" (48:35).

Righteous leaders will be present in the millennial kingdom. As noted in a previous lesson, Judah's leaders were a key reason as to why the people descended into idolatry. These leaders were corrupt, greedy, morally bankrupt, and led the people astray. However, Ezekiel's prophecy reveals the same will not be true in the millennial kingdom, for all its leaders will be righteous. This is especially true of the "prince," who will likely be a Davidic administrator of the kingdom during that time. Importantly, this prince will be a spiritual leader among the people: "It shall be the prince's part to give burnt offerings, grain offerings, and drink offerings, at the feasts, the New Moons, the Sabbaths, and at all the appointed seasons of the house of Israel" (45:17). Furthermore, other biblical texts reveal that believers in Christ will also participate in this administration: "And I saw thrones, and they sat on them, and judgment was committed to them. . . . And they lived and reigned with Christ for a thousand years" (Revelation 20:4).

Healing will take place in the millennial kingdom. In Ezekiel 47, the prophet describes the "healing" of the Dead Sea during the Millennium. In its current form, of course, the Dead Sea is quite dead. Because of its extreme salinity, nothing can live in its waters outside of a few microorganisms. However, during the Millennium, a river will run from underneath the temple that flows east and west. This river will empty into the Dead Sea—and a transformation will occur: "When it reaches the sea, its waters are healed. And it shall be that every living thing that moves, wherever the rivers go, will live. . . . Everything will live wherever the river goes" (47:8–9). Ezekiel adds, "[Trees] will bear fruit every month, because their water flows from the sanctuary. Their fruit will be for food, and their leaves for medicine" (verse 12). This picture of a physical healing of the land is representative of a larger restoration that will take place. Namely, our physical world and society itself will be restored to God's intended design. The presence of Christ will permeate the earth like the new river cleansing the Dead Sea.

REFLECTING ON THE TEXT

5) What does the Bible reveal about what it will be like to dwell with God in the millennial kingdom?

_____

_____

_____

_____

_____

_____

_____

6) Ungodly leaders caused great harm to the people of Judah in ancient times. Where have you seen the effects of good and bad leadership? According to Scripture, what makes someone a good leader?

_____

_____

_____

_____

_____

_____

7) How does good leadership in the church impact the lives of Christians? How would godly leadership in families and society influence our world today?

_____

_____

_____

_____

_____

_____

8) What do you most anticipate about the renewal God will bring to the world in the millennium?

_____

_____

_____

_____

_____

_____

_____

PERSONAL RESPONSE

9) Where do you currently have the opportunity to lead others in a way that is righteous?

_____

_____

_____

_____

_____

_____

10) What areas of your life are most in need of sanctification? (Pray that the Lord would work in your heart to restore you to His likeness.)

_____

_____

_____

_____

_____

_____

12

REVIEWING KEY PRINCIPLES

DRAWING NEAR

What have you appreciated or enjoyed the most about this study in the book of Ezekiel? What are some key principles that you have learned?

_____

_____

_____

_____

_____

_____

_____

_____

_____

_____

_____

_____

_____

_____

_____

_____

_____

_____

_____

_____

_____

THE CONTEXT

As we have seen, the role of God's prophets involved the past, present, and future. These prophets, Ezekiel included, were men and women of their times. They lived and ministered during a specific slice of history and addressed specific events that were important to the people of their day. They often spoke about the past, referencing God's covenants with Israel and His faithfulness throughout their history. They also often spoke about the future, describing both the reality of coming judgment and the promise of future blessing.

For these reasons and more, Ezekiel and his fellow prophets play a vital role in our understanding of the broader story of God's Word. They are crucial conduits that connect us with the ancient elements of God's dealings with humanity. They teach us important truths about our own relationship with God and how He desires us to live: "I will put a new spirit within them . . . that they may walk in My statutes and keep My judgments" (Ezekiel 11:19–20). They point us toward God's eternal promises, informing us that He has "thoughts of peace" for His people and plans to give them "a future and a hope" (Jeremiah 29:11).

Ezekiel, in particular, offers a wonderful (and detailed) view of the part of our future called the Millennium. Indeed, more details can be found about the thousand-year reign of Christ in Ezekiel 40–48 than anywhere else in the Bible—details about the temple and worship that will take place there, feasts of the Lord that will be celebrated, duties of the priests and "prince" who will serve as an administrator, land that will be set apart as a holy district, and land that will be distributed to the people of God. These chapters offered not only direct application to Ezekiel's original readers but also to followers of Christ in our world today.

EXPLORING THE MEANING

Glory is a key attribute of God's nature. One of the functions of the Bible is to reveal truths about God, including those about His nature. For example, we know from Scripture that God is love (see 1 John 4:7–8), that He is unchanging (see Malachi 3:6), that He is wise (see Romans 11:33), that He is good (see Psalm 34:8), that He is gracious and merciful (see Psalm 145:8), and that He is just (see Deuteronomy 32:4). In a similar way, the first chapter of Ezekiel offers a detailed glimpse into the aspect of God's nature that we call "glory." God is glorious, and He revealed that glory to Ezekiel through an incredible vision. Importantly, it is not that God *displayed* glory in this chapter or *acted* in ways that are glorious, for that would imply that God reflected something glorious that was outside of Himself. Instead, the text shows that God *is* glory. Glory is His nature, and that glory is sourced entirely in Him. Another way to express this truth is that we can only learn about glory (or experience it) by looking to God and studying Him as the source of all that is glorious.

All sin is a form of idolatry. The nation of Israel had been uniquely blessed and gifted with the revelation of God. They had been chosen for the specific purpose of revealing God to the rest of the world. Yet, for centuries, God's chosen people had ignored the reality of their calling and even rejected it. Rather than being a witness of God to the nations, they had turned to the religious practices of those nations. God's words in Ezekiel 5:7–8 are sobering: "Because you have multiplied disobedience more than the nations that are all around you. . . . Indeed I, even I, am against you and will execute judgments in your midst in the sight of the nations." Israel had rejected the true God and turned to false gods, which is idolatry. Similarly, all sin is rooted in idolatry. Even today, our sin is rooted in idolatry. Every time we turn away from God to serve something else—including our own desires or our own purposes—we are elevating that something else above God. We are practicing idolatry.

God knows those who belong to Him. Ezekiel 9 offers a "behind the scenes" view of the spiritual realm. While physically "seeing" Jerusalem in a vision, Ezekiel also witnessed six angelic beings charged with carrying out God's judgment against the city. Appearing as men, these angels each carried "a deadly weapon in his hand" (verse 1). One of the angels was given the task of identifying individuals in the city who still feared God. He was commanded to "mark" the foreheads of those who wept over the evil done there. The rest of the angels were given a chilling command: "Go after him through the city and kill; do not let your eye spare, nor have any pity. Utterly slay old and young men, maidens and little children and women; but do not come near anyone on whom is the mark" (verses 5–6). God's judgment against evil is always frightening, but the larger implication of this vision is encouraging for God's people—namely, He knows those who are His own. Even when we live within a wicked and corrupt culture, our Savior cares about and is faithful toward those who remain faithful to Him.

God loves His people intimately. In the church today, we often refer to God's "love" for His people. We describe how God loves His followers and how He loves the world. Yet if we are not careful, we can drift into thinking of God's love in general (or even generic) terms. Ezekiel 16, however, reveals that God's love is deeply intimate. Through His prophet, God described His love for Israel in terms of someone finding an abandoned baby and choosing to embrace it as a beloved child. The language here is deeply personal: "'When I passed by you again and looked upon you, indeed your time was the time of love; so I spread My wing over you and covered your nakedness. Yes, I swore an oath to you and entered into a covenant with you, and you became Mine,' says the Lord GOD" (verse 8). Because God is the same yesterday, today, and forever, we know that He draws near to us with this same intimate, personal love.

God's methods of judgment are just. The captives living in Babylon had apparently begun to feel that God was treating them unjustly. They quoted a proverb implying that God was punishing them because of the transgressions of earlier generations: "The fathers have eaten sour grapes, and the children's teeth are set on edge" (Ezekiel 18:2). God rejected these claims and, in so doing, established a critical principle: people are judged on their individual faith and conduct toward Him, not on the nation in which they live or the community into which they were born. "'If [a man] has walked in My statutes and kept My judgments faithfully—he is just; he shall surely live!' says the Lord GOD" (verse 9). Conversely, if someone chooses to reject God and embrace a life of oppression, violence, greed, and other forms of idolatry, "he shall surely die; his blood shall be upon him" (verse 13).

Do not put your trust in anything of this world. In Ezekiel 28, God directed His prophet to describe the king of Tyre using language and imagery that can also be connected to Satan. For instance, in one place Ezekiel writes of the king, "You were the seal of perfection, full of wisdom and perfect in beauty. You were in Eden, the garden of God" (verses 12–13). Similarly, he writes, "You were the anointed cherub who covers; I established you; you were on the holy mountain of God" (verse 14). By making a direct link between Satan and the king of Tyre—a pagan and rebellious nation—God was revealing Satan to be the power behind that king. Satan had fueled the rise of Tyre as an enemy of God's people and had directly influenced her king to thwart God's plans. Importantly, the descriptions in Ezekiel 28:1–19 *do* apply to the human person who ruled as the king of Tyre and are not allegorical. However, these verses contain multiple layers in that they also highlight Satan's influence in the lives of all people who choose to make themselves an enemy of God. In the end, all the plans of such people will fail (see Psalm 37:12–15), just as all the plans of Satan will ultimately come to destruction.

God desires His people to repent. The crisis highlighted thus far in Ezekiel is that God's people had rejected Him and pursued the gods and lifestyles of the pagan nations. Their choices had put them on a pathway to ruin—a pathway God wanted them to avoid. He desired His people to listen to Ezekiel (and the other prophets) and *repent* of their sins. God had heard the people of Judah asking, "If our transgressions and our sins lie upon us, and we pine away in them, how can we then live?" (33:10). The Lord gave this answer through Ezekiel: "Turn, turn from your evil ways! For why should you die, O house of Israel?" (verse 11). This same pattern has been repeated throughout human history. When people seek to remain sovereign over their own lives, they steer themselves toward destruction. God's desire is to warn all people away from that destruction and for them to repent. In the words of Peter: "The Lord is not slack concerning His promise, as some count slackness, but is longsuffering toward us, not willing that any should perish but that all should come to repentance" (2 Peter 3:9).

God brings the promise of the Holy Spirit. One of the key factors involved in the restoration of Israel would be the pouring out of the Holy Spirit. In Ezekiel 36, the Lord described a when/then scenario: "I will put My Spirit within you and cause you to walk in My statutes, and you will keep My judgments and do them. Then you shall dwell in the land that I gave to your fathers; you shall be My people, and I will be your God" (verses 27–28). *When* God placed His Spirit within Israel, *then* they would dwell in the land. In Ezekiel 37, God again declared, "I will put My Spirit in you, and you shall live, and I will place you in your own land." (verse 14). In the same way that God poured out His Spirit to launch the church (see Acts 2:1–4), He will one day pour out His Spirit on Israel before fully restoring that nation during Christ's millennial kingdom.

God desires all His people to return to Him. It is worth asking why Ezekiel received this extended vision of the temple at this specific moment in his people's history. We know from the text that Ezekiel's vision took place "in the fourteenth year after the city was captured" (40:1). Thus, one reason for the timing of the vision was to offer hope to the captives—to reveal a future time in which everything they had lost would be restored and even improved. However, God identified a second reason: "Son of man, describe the temple to the house of Israel, that they may be ashamed of their iniquities; and let them measure the pattern. And if they are ashamed of all that they have done, make known to them the design of the temple and its arrangement, its exits and its entrances, its entire design and all its ordinances, all its forms and all its laws" (43:10–11). God wanted His people to acknowledge that they had rebelled against Him. He then wanted them to repent of their sins and fully return to Him.

UNLEASHING THE TEXT

1) Which of the themes discussed in your study of Ezekiel did you enjoy most? Why?

_____

_____

_____

_____

_____

2) What did you find challenging throughout this study? What did you find most rewarding?

_____

_____

_____

_____

_____

3) How has your study of Ezekiel helped you better understand God's nature and character?

_____

_____

_____

_____

_____

4) Why is the promise of the future reign of Christ during the Millennium an important element of your spiritual life today?

_____
_____
_____
_____
_____
_____
_____

PERSONAL RESPONSE

5) Have you repented of your sin and placed your faith in the finished work of Jesus Christ? Do you strive to put off sin and put on righteousness out of love for Him? Explain your response.

_____
_____
_____
_____
_____
_____
_____

6) What sins have you been most convicted of during this study? What will you do to address these sins? What will that look like over time? Be specific.

_____
_____
_____
_____
_____
_____

7) What steps will you take to share what you have learned throughout this study with others who need to hear it?

_____

_____

_____

_____

_____

_____

_____

_____

_____

8) In what areas do you hope to grow spiritually over the coming weeks and months? What steps will you need to take in order to achieve that growth?

_____

_____

_____

_____

_____

_____

_____

_____

_____

If you would like to continue in your study of the Old Testament, read the next title in this series: *Daniel & Esther: Israel in Exile.*

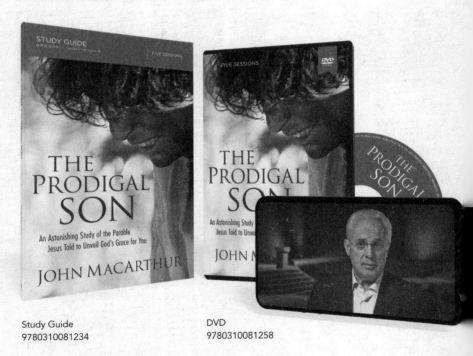

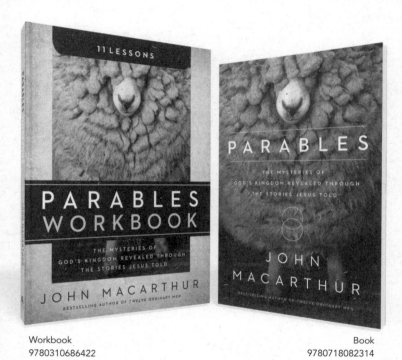

From the Publisher

GREAT STUDIES

ARE EVEN BETTER WHEN THEY'RE SHARED!

Help others find this study:

- Post a review at your favorite online bookseller.

- Post a picture on a social media account and share why you enjoyed it.

- Send a note to a friend who would also love it—or, better yet, go through it with them!

Thanks for helping others grow their faith!